Used to Play Guitar

Start Playing Again Today—You'll Be Surprised What You Remember!

Jody Fisher

...fred, the leader in educational publishing, and

...e National Guitar Workshop, one of America's

...nest guitar schools, have joined forces to bring

...ou the best, most progressive educational tools

...ossible. We hope you will enjoy this book and

...ncourage you to look for other fine products

...om Alfred and the National Guitar Workshop.

...s book was acquired, edited and produced by
...orkshop Arts, Inc., the publishing arm of
... National Guitar Workshop
...thaniel Gunod: editor
...an Benison: music typesetter
...othy Phelps: interior design
... Recorded at Studio 9, Pomona, CA
...ver photograph courtesy of Taylor Guitars

Table of Contents

Track 1

This book is accompanied by a compact disc. Using this CD will help make learning more enjoyable and the information more meaningful. It will help you play the correct notes and rhythms of each example. The track numbers below the symbols correspond directly to the example you want to hear. Have fun!

About the Author

Jody Fisher has worked professionally in virtually all styles of music during his career, from straight-ahead and contemporary jazz to rock'n'roll, country and pop. He taught Guitar and Jazz Studies at both the University of Redlands and Idyllwild School of Music and the Arts (ISOMATA). An active performer in the Southern California area, he maintains a private teaching practice and is a director of the National Guitar Workshop.

Other instructional products by Jody Fisher:

30-Day Guitar Workout
Beginning Jazz Guitar (video)
Chord and Scale Finder
Ear Training for the Contemporary Guitarist
Jazz Guitar Christmas
Jazz Guitar Masterclass
      (with Joe Diorio, Mark Whitfield,
      Ron Escheté, Scott Henderson
      and Steve Khan)
Jazz Skills
Rhythm Guitar Encyclopedia
Stand Alone Tracks: Smooth Jazz
The Complete Jazz Guitar Method:
      Beginning Jazz Guitar
      Intermediate Jazz Guitar
      Mastering Jazz Guitar: Chord/Melody
      Mastering Jazz Guitar: Improvisation
The Guitar Mode Encyclopedia
Jazz Guitar Harmony
The Art of Solo Guitar, Book 1
The Art of Solo Guitar, Book 2

Introduction

The purpose of this book is to reacquaint you with an old friend. Although a guitar is an inanimate object, most of us who play and spend time with our guitars know that it is indeed a friend—and a pretty close one at that.

This book is for adults who have played the guitar at some point in their lives and, for whatever reason, stopped playing. Careers, family obligations or even just the hectic pace of life are the usual reasons for leaving this old friend behind. But once a guitar player, always a guitar player. Somewhere in the back of our minds we remember the good times, the challenges and the sense of accomplishment from spending time with the guitar. The thought "I'll get back to it eventually" never seems to leave us completely. This is true whether you prefer playing rock, folk or blues music on either an acoustic or electric guitar.

Here is your chance to be reintroduced to the skills and information you once knew. You'll likely be surprised how fast it all comes back to you. It's simply a matter of clearing the cobwebs from your mind and limbering up your fingers.

This book covers basic chords and some more challenging ones as well. Strumming, flatpicking and fingerpicking are also discussed. You will learn the basics of improvising over most styles of popular music. If you once read standard music notation you'll be reminded of that, or if you ever wanted to learn to do it, you'll get the chance for that, too.

If your goal is to play like you used to, you will find help here. If you aspire to take your playing even farther, you'll find that information here as well. I think you will find a relaxed, no-pressure approach to just having fun with the guitar.

Most importantly, you'll have the chance to hang out with that old friend of yours again.

Part 1: Your Guitar

Let's face it—your guitar is a very personal possession and you are going to spend quite a bit of time with it. Besides practicing, and possibly performing for family and friends, you will probably take time polishing, changing strings, maintaining and maybe just admiring your guitar. Since it may have been some time since you last played, you should be aware that some things about guitars could have changed. You may also need a refresher course on the care and feeding of your instrument. We won't be discussing anything too complicated or technical, but knowing some of the basics can definitely enhance your enjoyment.

Types of Guitars

Nylon-String Guitars

Nylon-string guitars are often called *classical* guitars. While it is true that all true classical guitars have nylon strings, many are manufactured with other uses in mind. These days, nylon-string guitars can be electrified, or not. Some have cutaways and much narrower necks than traditional classical guitars. There are even semi-acoustic and solid-body nylon-string guitars. Guitars with nylon strings are perfect if you are going to play fingerstyle and desire a warmer, softer sound. Some players even use a pick with these guitars.

Steel-String Acoustic Guitars

Steel-string acoustic guitars are used universally in all kinds of music. The sound of these guitars can be heard in rock, pop, blues, country, folk, fingerstyle and jazz. Steel-string acoustics come in many sizes and styles, from smaller parlor-size instruments to full-size jumbos. Many are electrified with pickups set into (or under) the string saddles. Most of these guitars have sound holes on the top but some have "f-holes" instead.

Electric Solid Body Guitars

Solidbody guitars are made from a solid piece of wood. The sounds and shapes of Stratocaster-, Telecaster- and Les Paul-style guitars are well known. There are many other styles to choose from as well. If you are into rock, in most cases you should be playing a solid body guitar, although any style of music can be played on them.

Electric Hollow Body Guitars

The bodies of these instruments are hollow but are electrified in much the same way as the solid bodies. Generally, larger hollow bodies are intended for softer music such as jazz, because they tend to feed back through the amplifier at higher volumes. Thinline-style hollow bodies generally don't have this problem. Some of these guitars have a block of wood inside the body to keep the feedback problem under control. This usually works quite well for players that want a more "hollow" sound but still want to play a variety of musical styles.

Taking Care of Your Guitar

Strings

There are now endless varieties of strings available. When you buy a new guitar, plan on experimenting a little with different brands and gauges. Broadly speaking, sets of strings come in light, medium and heavy gauges. Different manufacturers have varying definitions of what actually constitutes the various gauges, so deciding what strings are right for your guitar is sometimes a matter of trial and error. Strings can be made from nickel, bronze, stainless steel and many other compounds. They are also wound in a variety of ways, such as roundwound, flatwound, semi-round and tape-wrapped. Nylon strings are generally described as "medium" or "high" tension. In general, the lowest three strings have a metal wrapping, although some sets also have one additional wrapped string.

String Tips

1. Always wipe your strings off when you are done playing. Perspiration and other acids from your skin can adversely affect the string's longevity.

2. When not playing, keep your guitar in its case. The air can oxidize the strings rapidly.

3. Don't wait for strings to break before you change them. Your string's life expectancy depends on how much you play, body chemistry, your technique and your environment. When they start to sound a little dead—change them.

4. Keep your guitar tuned to pitch (A = 440, see Tuning, page 8).

Picks

Picks come in all shapes, weights and sizes. Try not to use any pick that is too large or picks that seem "gimmicky." This is not a huge investment, so purchase a few dollars worth of picks, experiment and see what you like.

The Setup

"Setting up" a guitar refers to making sure the guitar is easy to play and plays perfectly in tune. Most guitars shipped from the factory need setting up. Some guitar shops set them up before selling them and others don't. The simplest setups involve the *bridge*, the *trussrod*, the *saddles* and the *nut*. It is advisable to have a professional guitar repair person or luthier make these adjustments.

The bridge moves up and down and adjusts the height of the strings above the fretboard. Some players prefer lower action and others like the feel of higher action. It is sometimes a question of comfort or tone. Higher action normally produces a better sound while lower action usually feels more comfortable; most players look for the perfect spot right in between.

The trussrod is a metal apparatus inside the neck that can adjust the "relief" of the fingerboard. The trussrod can slightly bend the neck to bring the surface of the fretboard closer, or farther away from the strings.

The saddles (one for each string on many electric guitars) are found right on top of the bridge. They move forward and backward to adjust string length. Proper adjustment of the saddles will ensure correct intonation and tuning along the entire fingerboard. Many guitars have one saddle for all six strings. The nut is at the head of the guitar, just below the 1st fret. It creates the space between each string and can also be filed so that the strings lie closer to the frets.

Taking the time to make sure your guitar is set up properly will make picking it up again much more enjoyable. For more information about setting up and maintaining a guitar, check out *Guitar Shop: Setup and Maintenance* by John Carruthers (National Guitar Workshop/Alfred #18479).

Cleaning

Dusting the entire guitar with a cloth is usually sufficient. When you want to polish it, use a product that is made specifically for guitars. There are many available. Use a soft, lint-free cloth and polish sparingly. Do not polish the fretboard. If you must clean the fretboard, use just a dab of lighter fluid on a soft cloth and rub lightly. Don't do this too frequently, as the lighter fluid can dry out the wood.

Tuning

The strings can be tuned to a piano, a tuner or to one another. To tune to a piano, match the strings to the keys as shown at the right. To tune the strings to each other, first tune the 6th string to an external source, such as the piano and then follow Steps 1 through 6 shown on the right. Start from the lowest sounding strings and work up to the highest. Play an open string, then play the matching note on the next lower string. Tune the open string up or down until the notes match exactly.

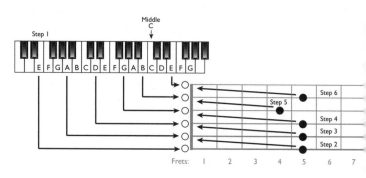

Tuning takes practice, and you may want to enlist the help of an experienced player. It is important that the note "A" on the guitar (5th fret, 1st string) sound at 440 cycles per second, which is called *concert pitch*. Guitars and guitar strings are designed to sound their best when tuned at concert pitch.

Parts of the Guitar

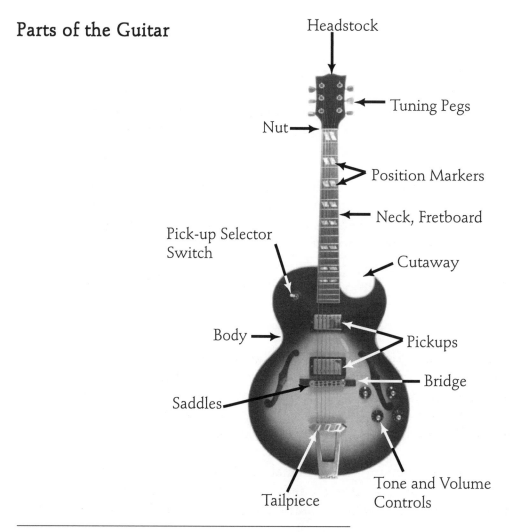

Part 2: Chords

Basic Open-Position Chords

When you first started playing the guitar, you very likely learned quite a few of the chords covered in this chapter. While some of these fingerings are a little more challenging than others, you will find that most are quite simple. Since you have played before, the learning curve on these should be pretty fast. The most common open-position chords are included here and after you get a feel for them, there are literally thousands of songs you'll be able to play in many different styles of music. We call these *open-position* chords because they usually include open strings and are found below the 5th fret. If you want to learn more chords like these, you should pick up a chord encyclopedia (such as *The Ultimate Guitar Chord Bible*, NGW #07-1083, or *The Guitar Chord Encyclopedia*, Alfred #4440). Learning new songs is a great way to learn new chords.

Chords will be shown to you on fretboard diagrams such as this.

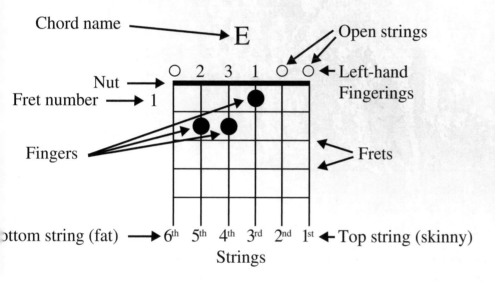

The fingers on your "chording" hand are numbered as follows.

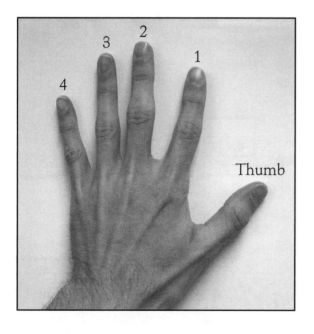

Before you start learning these chords you may need to be reminded of a few technical considerations.

- Use a strap. The strap frees your hands from holding the instrument so you can play more easily.

- Sit or stand comfortably, but try to keep your back straight. This will aid your progress.

- Always try to use your fingertips when making chords. Avoid playing with the pads of your fingers.

- Place your fingers directly behind the fret wires.

- In most cases, your thumb should remain behind the neck. This is much easier if you are using a strap.

The following chords come from the three largest families of chords.

Major
> We use only the letter name for major chords (C = C Major)

Minor
> We add a lower case "min" to designate minor chords (Cmin = C Minor). Many books will use just "m."

Dominant
> The true name for the chords with a "7" is "dominant 7" (C7 = C Dominant 7). We shorten it to "7" to make life a little easier.

Major Chords

A

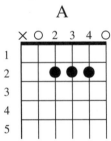

B

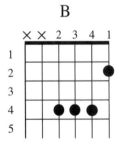

C

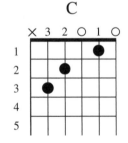

D

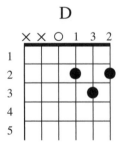

E

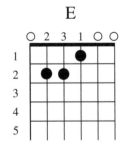

F

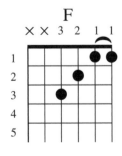

G

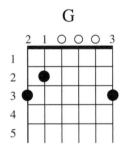

$\overset{1\frown 1}{\bullet\bullet}$ = *Barre.* One finger covers more than one string.

× = String not included in chord.

inor Chords

Amin
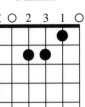

Bmin
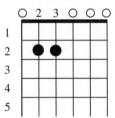

Cmin
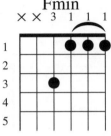

Dmin
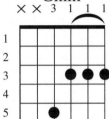

Emin
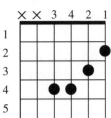

Fmin
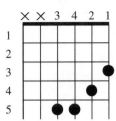

Gmin
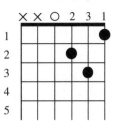

Chords

A7

B7
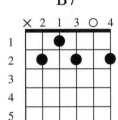

C7
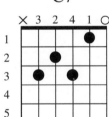

D7
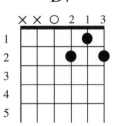

E7
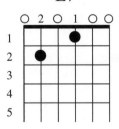

F7
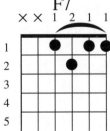

G7
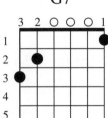

Learning Chords

You may remember that learning chords is sort of a two-step process. First, you have to learn the chord itself, then you have to learn to change from one chord to another. Here are a couple of shortcuts.

1. When learning a new chord, try to play the chord and then hold it in position for 30 seconds (give or take a few). Do this several times. This helps both your brain and your muscle memory to learn what you are trying to accomplish.

2. Most people try to move all of their fingers at once when changing from one chord to another. This is exactly what you are supposed to do—once you are able. In the early stages of learning, however, this can be difficult. The first step is to learn what each finger is doing individually. Once you are fully aware of where each finger is going to go, moving them simultaneously becomes much easier.

Strumming Chords

You will learn various strumming patterns as you progress through this book. Some will be familiar and others may be new to you. For now, strum using only *downstrokes* (strum down, toward the floor). This will let you concentrate on your left hand.

Hold the pick between your thumb and index finger and assertively strum downward, making sure you are striking only the strings contained in the chord.

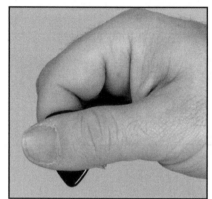

Hold the pick between your thumb and index finger.

Try to keep an even and steady beat. In the examples below, a slash mark (╱) represents a single downstroke.

The following chord *progressions* (series of chords) provide a great opportunity for working on your chord playing skills. Thousands of songs are based on these progressions. By working on them now, you will make the process of learning actual songs simpler.

If you find that any progression is a little too difficult for you, don't worry. Just move on to a different one. You can learn these in any order you like.

ny songs have chord progressions with only two chords. If you don't read music, don't worry.
you need to know for now is that music is divided into *measures* (groups of beats) by *bar*
es. **C** is the symbol used for common time, which means there are four beats per measure.
eans there are three beats per measure. See Part 3 (page 51) in this book for a more in-depth
k at reading music.

gressions with Major Chords

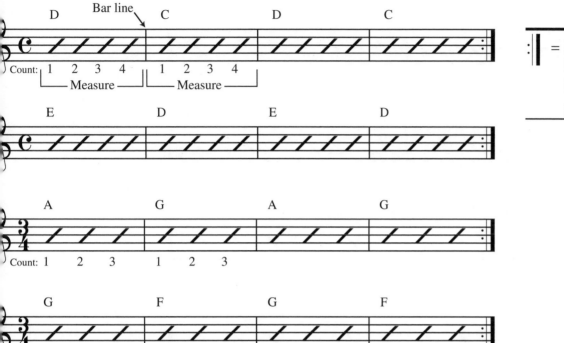

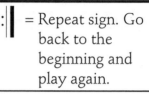
= Repeat sign. Go back to the beginning and play again.

gressions with Major and Minor Chords

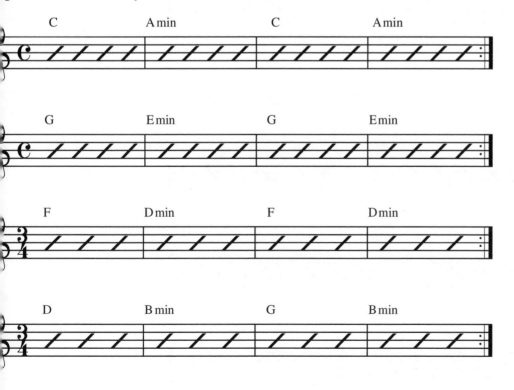

Progressions with 7 Chords and Major Chords

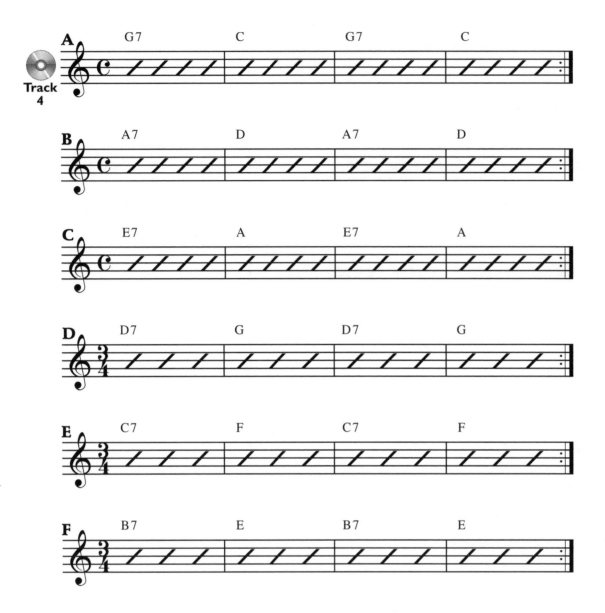

The 12-Bar Blues

Many blues and rock songs are based on these *12-bar blues* progressions.

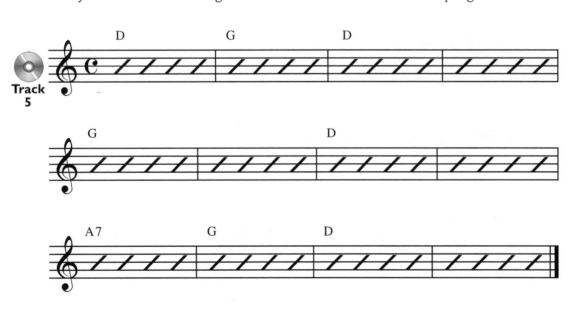

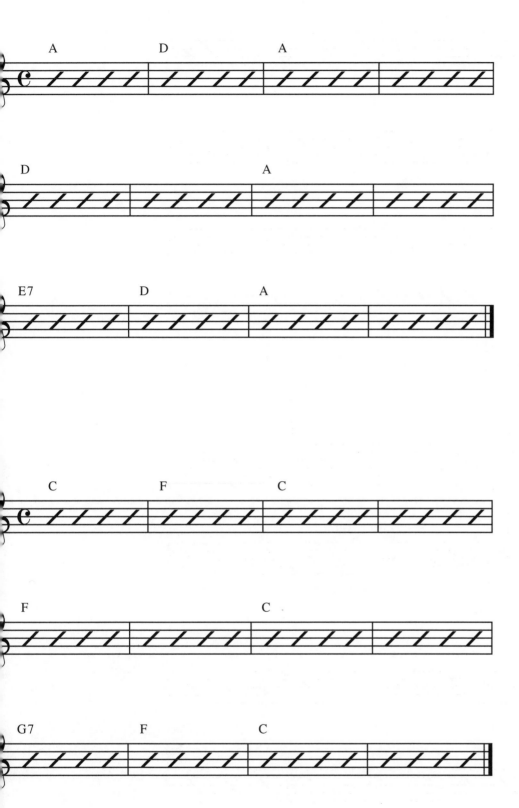

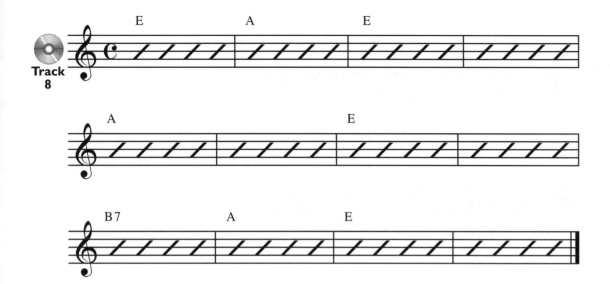

Other Common Progressions

Many pop songs and oldies from the 1950s and '60s are based on these progressions.

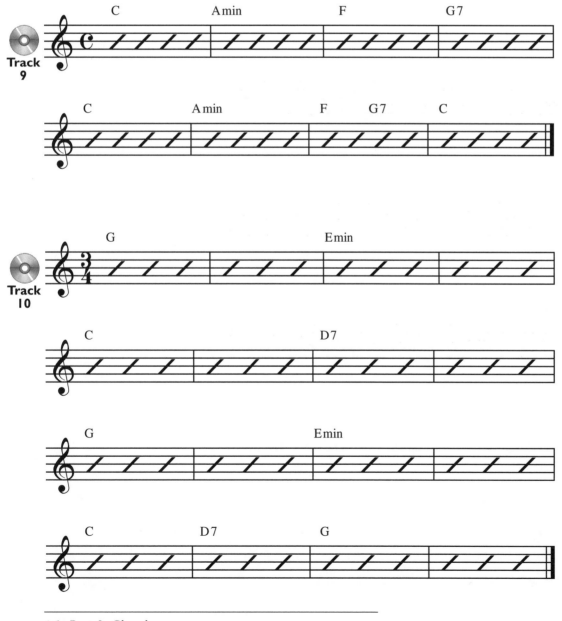

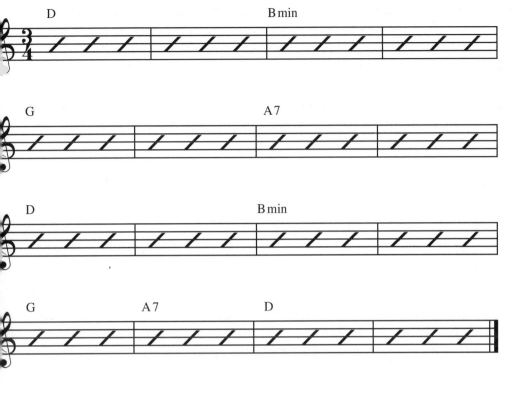

ounting Time

ne of the most important musical skills you can develop is the ability to maintain a steady beat. ost songs should begin and end at exactly the same *tempo* (speed). This is not that easy to do, pecially if you have never worked on it before. After some practice, this can become auto- atic.

hen listening to others play we often find ourselves tapping our foot to keep time with the usic. When you are the one performing the music, it is *your* job to set the pace of the song. fore you begin a song or exercise, take a moment to set the tempo internally. While playing, p your foot. As in the previous pages, progressions are often shown containing slash marks / the measures. Each slash represents one beat. For our current purposes, we will consider a beat ual to one tap of the foot.

sure you are able to play the song (or exercise) at the tempo you are setting. It is common for experienced players to start out too fast. Watch out for this—it could cause you to slow down for e difficult parts of the song and speed up on the easier sections, thereby disrupting the tempo. member, the idea is to end the song at the same tempo at which you started *without* nwanted fluctuations.

the best you can. It can take a little time to develop good chord-playing skills, but you will prove after a while. Some people like to practice with a *metronome* (an adjustable device hich provides a steady click to play with) which can help, but eventually you should be able to ep good time without one.

would be a good idea to go over the last few pages of progressions and play them again with ese ideas in mind.

Strumming Rhythms

Now it's time to dress up our strumming a little. Playing a song using only downstrokes can get tiresome pretty quickly. This section will show a variety of strumming *rhythms* (patterns of long and short durations). Before we get to them, we should talk a little more about how these are represented in a piece of music.

These symbols, called *quarter-note strums*, represent one-beat strums. Thus far, we have used simple slashes. Both symbols are used, but the slashes can often mean "any rhythm you want here." The quarter-note strum symbol is more specifc.

Quarter-Note Strums

Count: 1   2   3   4

In the previous examples there were strums on each beat of the measure. Sometimes we need to let a chord ring for more than just one beat. The following symbols, called *half-note strums*, represent strummed chords that ring for two beats each (or two foot taps).

Half-Note Strums

Count: 1   2   3   4

Try your hand at playing these progressions in the rhythms shown.

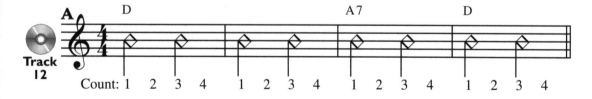

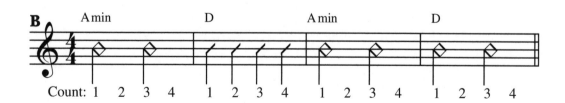

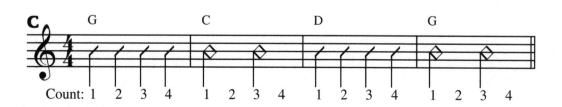

hen you see a *dot* next to a half-note strum, let the chord ring for three beats. This is called a *dotted half-note strum.*

Dotted Half-Note Strum

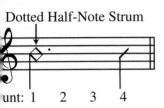

unt: 1   2   3   4

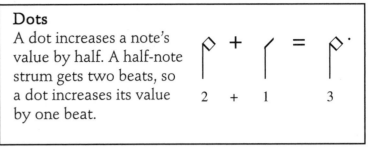

Dots
A dot increases a note's value by half. A half-note strum gets two beats, so a dot increases its value by one beat.

ere are some more practice progressions using dotted half-note strums.

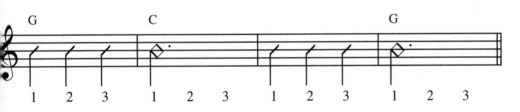

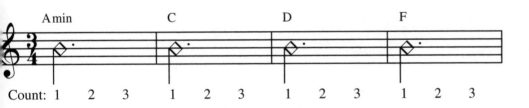

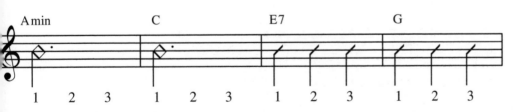

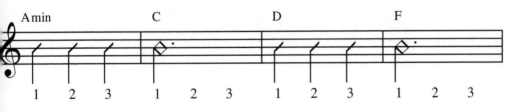

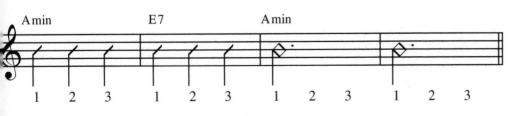

The *whole-note strum* symbol represents a chord that is held for four beats:

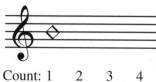

Whole-Note Strum

Count: 1   2   3   4

Here are some chord progressions to practice that utilize the whole-note strum.

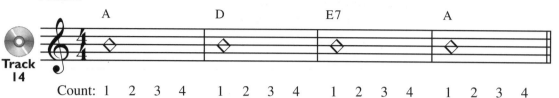

Sometimes we need to play two strums—one downstroke and one upstroke (toward the ceiling)—in a single beat. These are called *eighth-note strums*. These aren't difficult but some explanation is necessary.

ne foot tap actually consists of two different motions: a
wnward motion bringing your foot to the floor and an
ward motion bringing your foot back up in preparation
r the next tap. To play two strums in a single beat, we
mply strum once on the tap and once at the top of the
ward motion. Practice the following exercises until this feels

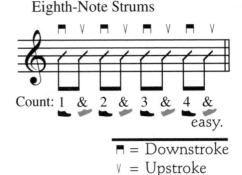

easy.

actice these progressions with eighth-note strums.

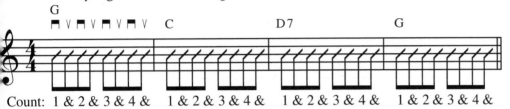

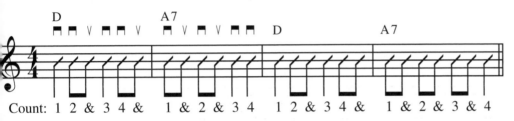

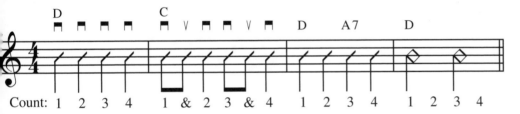

trumming Rhythms with Rests

/e also use signs to indicate periods of silence—when we don't strum at all. These signs are
lled *rests*. This chart shows the rests along with their corresponding notes.

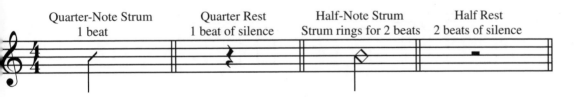

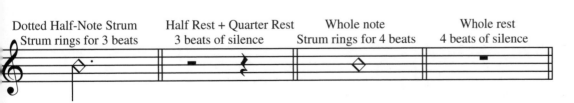

Practice these exercises that incorporate rests. To perform the rests, use either your left-hand fingers or the right side of your right hand to stop the vibrations of the strings.

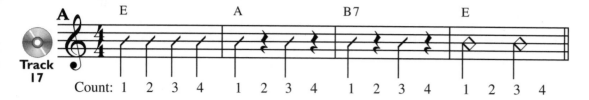

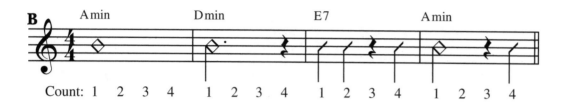

Common Strumming Rhythms

If you can play the previous exercises without too much difficulty, then you are ready to learn some of these common strumming patterns. You will find these useful for playing a wide variety of songs in various styles. Not all patterns will fit all situations. It is up to you to discover which sounds and feels right for a particular song.

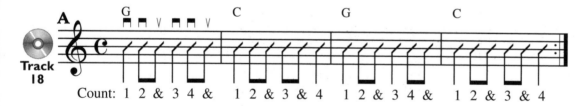

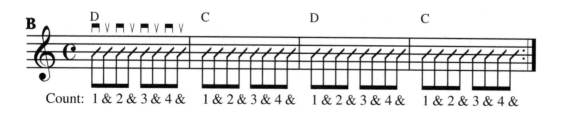

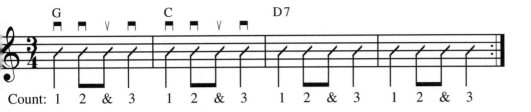

Count: 1　2　&　3　　　1　2　&　3　　　1　2　&　3　　　1　2　&　3

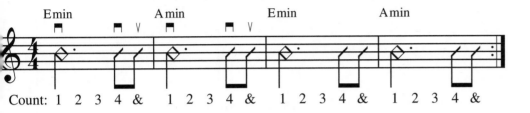

Count: 1　2　3　4　&　　　1　2　3　4　&　　　1　2　3　4　&　　　1　2　3　4　&

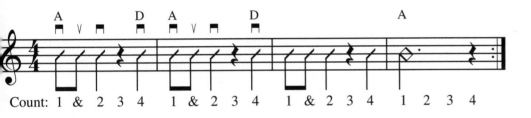

Count: 1　&　2　3　4　　　1　&　2　3　4　　　1　&　2　3　4　　　1　2　3　4

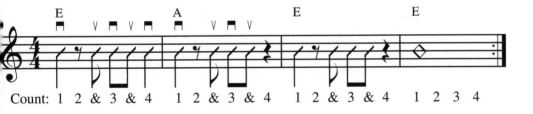

Count: 1　2　&　3　&　4　　　1　2　&　3　&　4　　　1　2　&　3　&　4　　　1　2　3　4

Barre Chords

Now that your strumming skills are returning and your left-hand fingers are getting used to playing chords again, it's time to get back into *barre* chords. You probably remember this challenge from the first time around. When guitar students learn new chord shapes, the tendency is to use brute strength to hold the strings down. Here's a secret for you: Strength really doesn't have a lot to do with sounding any chord! Most often it's a matter of finger placement and balance.

Here are a few tips for learning barre chords:

1. Keep your thumb behind the neck. This way you can actually press the strings *between* your thumb and index finger.

2. Often you will be more successful if you place your other fingers down *before* you make your barre.

3. Relax into the chord—you really don't have to press too hard. Just press firmly and confidently. You will find this much easier to learn the second time around. Your muscle memory will kick in again with just a little coaxing.

Moveable and Stationary Chords

Most of the open-position chords you learned a few pages back fall into a category called *stationary* chords. That is, they usually can only be played in the position in which you learned them because they contain open strings. Some of these chord shapes actually do sound okay when you start sliding them around the fretboard, but most of them will not.

Moveable chords have shapes that allow you to play them anywhere on the fretboard. There are many advantages to this. With open-position chords, you must learn a new shape for every chord you learn. With moveable barre chords, a single chord shape can be used to produce many different chords. Moveable barre chords also add a certain consistency to the sound. Once you know how they are organized on the guitar, you'll find that changing from one barre chord to another can be easier than changing all the various shapes found in open-position chords.

Barre chords don't necessarily take the place of open-position chords. Open-position chords produce a beautiful and distinctive sound that is unique to them *because* of the open strings involved. Barre chords give you an easy system to work with that produces a tighter sound that is perfect for rock and other forms of popular music.

ots on the 6th String

u are about to learn two different sets of barre chords. The *roots* (white circles) of the chords in
first set will all be found on the 6th string. A root is the note which gives a chord its letter
ne, such as the A in an A chord, the C in a C7 chord or the E in an Emin chord.

re are the chord shapes with roots on the 6th string.

Major	Minor	Dominant 7	Dominant 7

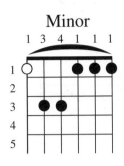
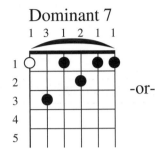
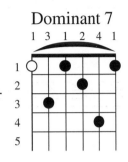

u can see that by simply adding or removing various fingers from the major shape, we
oduce either a minor or dominant 7 shape.

re's the cool part: The diagram on the left shows the notes along the 6th string. By moving
e above shapes up and down the neck, we travel from root to root. In other words, playing the
jor shape at the 3rd fret produces a G Major chord. Sliding it up to the 7th fret produces a
Major chord, and so on. Of course, the same idea applies when sliding minor and dominant 7
apes around as well.

String Roots

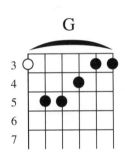

G   B

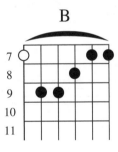

$\underline{\overline{\text{O}}}$ = Root

* Any *sharp* ♯ name can also be
called by a *flat* ♭ name. These are
called *enharmonic equivalents.* As
you may recall, a sharp raises a
note by one fret, a flat lowers a
note by one fret.

Gmin   Bmin

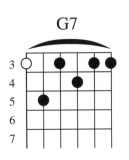

G7 B7   G7 B7

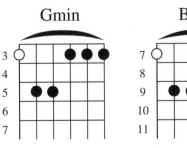
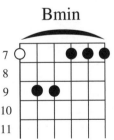
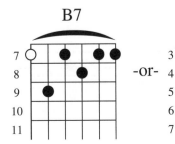
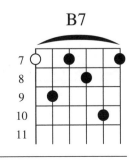

-or-

Following are chord progressions to help you memorize where these barre chords are found. Remember, the slashes can now be interpreted as "any rhythm you want here." Be creative with your strumming!

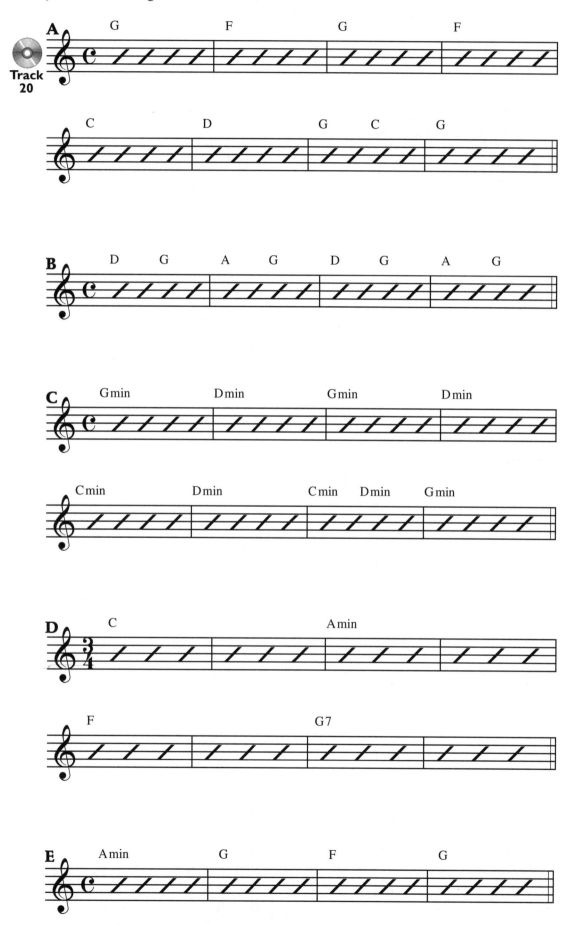

is exercise will take you through all of the major barre chords.

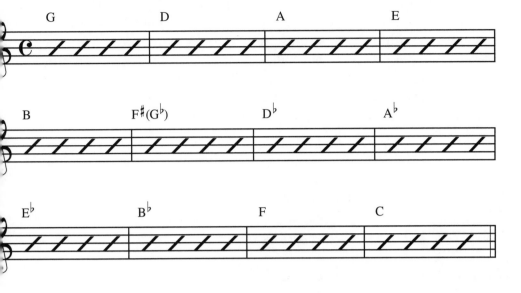

re it is again, this time with major and minor barre chords.

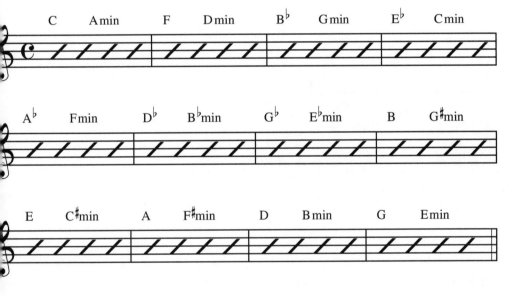

is one mixes major, minor and dominant 7 barre chords.

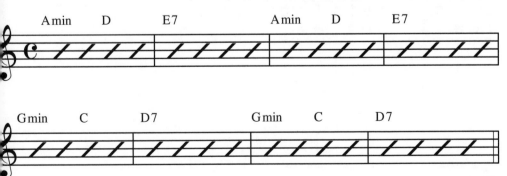

Roots on the 5th String

Here is the second set of barre chord shapes with roots found on the 5th string. There is something else that makes this set different from the first set: these chords do not use all six strings. The major chord is found on the middle four strings only. If you let your 3rd finger touch the first string very lightly—which will happen quite naturally—you will find that you can mute the sound of that string. You can also use your 1st finger to mute the sound of the 6th string for the major chord. This way you don't have to be so careful about strumming only the middle four strings. Both the minor and dominant 7 shapes use the top five strings. Mute the 6th string on these as well.

Major
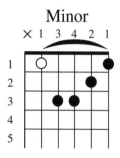

Minor
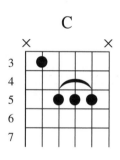

Dominant 7
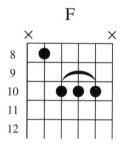

5th String Roots
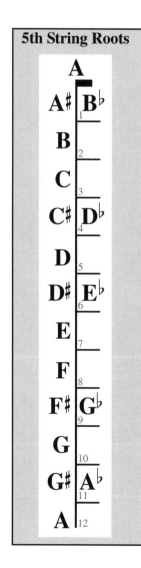

C
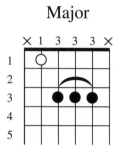

F
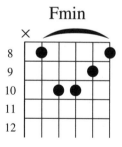

Cmin
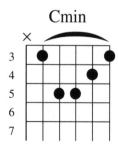

Fmin
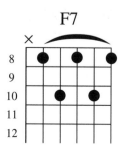

C7
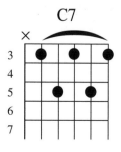

F7

...ctice the barre chords with roots on the 5th string in the following exercises.

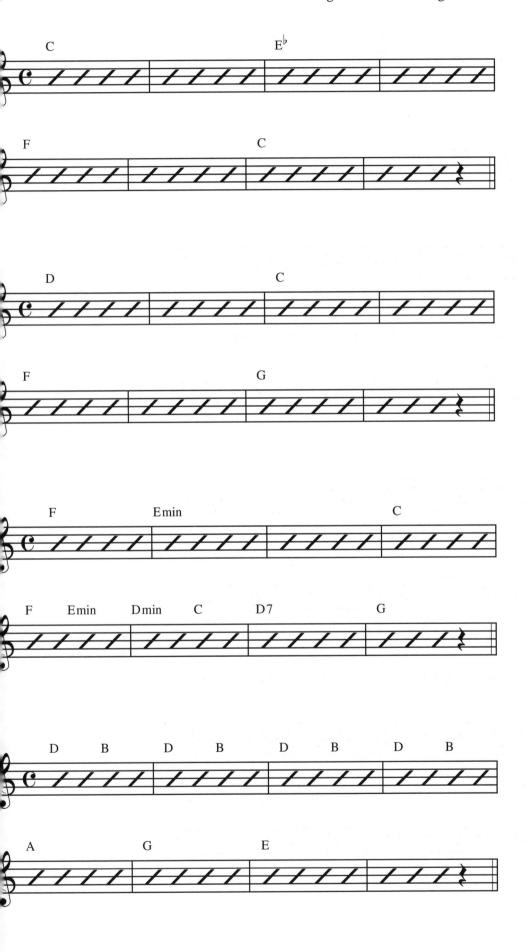

This exercise will take you through all the major chords. Use only barre chords with roots on the 5th string.

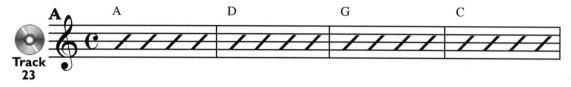

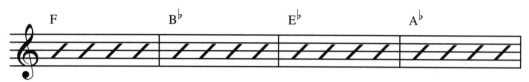

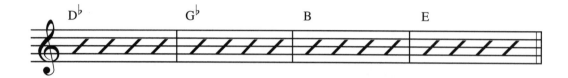

This one will give your major and minor chords with roots on the 5th string a workout.

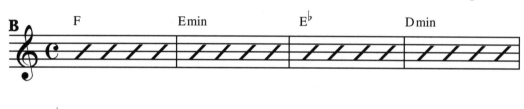

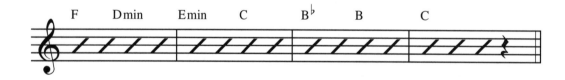

This exercise uses major, minor and dominant 7 chords with roots on the 5th string.

Choosing Which Type of Barre to Use

After practicing the previous progressions with both kinds of barre chords—those with roots on the 6th string and those with roots on the 5th string—you have undoubtedly noticed that each chord can be played in two different places.

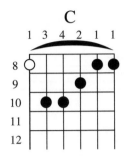 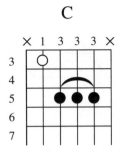

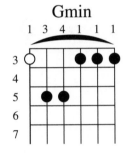 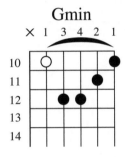

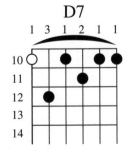 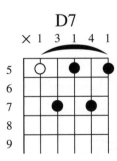

Does it make a difference which type of barre you use in an actual song? It depends. Sometimes a chord is chosen because of its sound. Other times it's more a matter of convenience. You could play the following progression several ways. Even though the chord names are the same, they all sound slightly different.

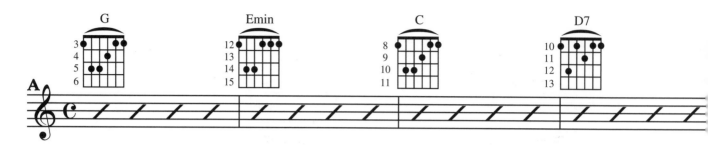

-or-

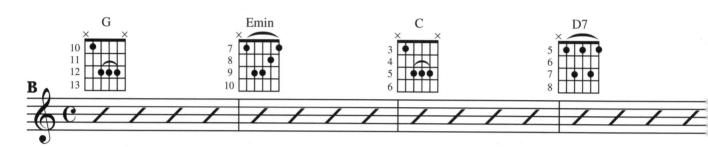

-or-

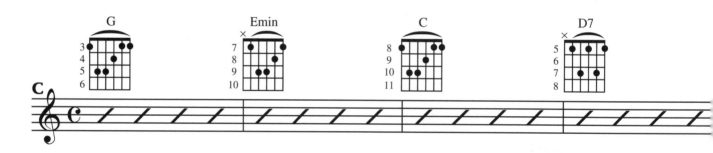

-or-

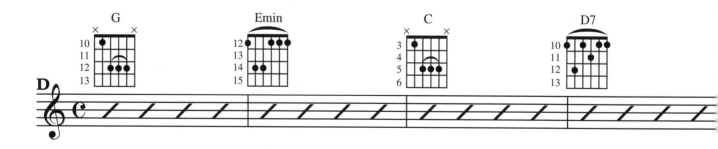

Here is another example of a progression played several different ways.

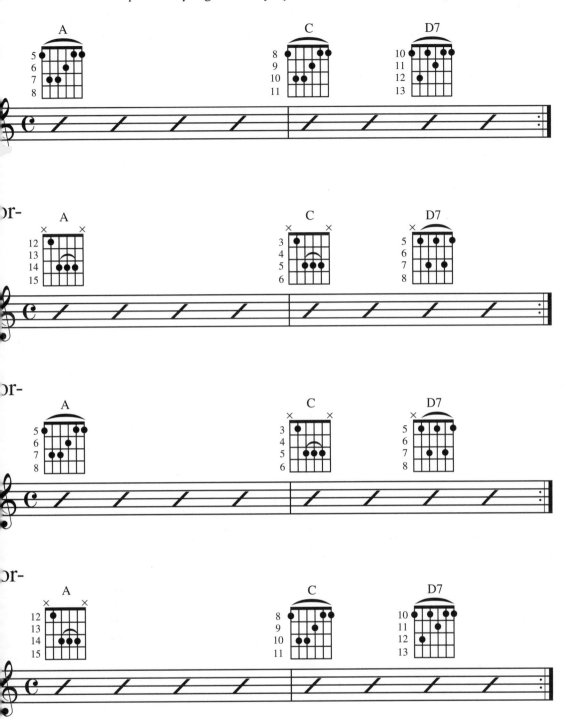

As you can see, it's really up to you which type of barre you choose for any given chord. Sometimes it's easier to keep the chords in close proximity to each other. Other times you may prefer the sound of the chords moving move up and down the neck.

Reading Tablature

Tablature is a graphic system of illustrating where to play notes on the guitar fretboard. It is literally a diagram of the strings with instructions on where to place your fingers. While handy at times, it should not be considered a substitute for reading standard music notation, but until you are able to do so, using tablature is perfectly alright.

Up to this point, you have been dusting off your chord and strumming skills. Learning the basics of reading tablature (or TAB) will allow you to advance to more interesting ways of playing.

TAB uses six parallel horizontal lines. The lowest line represents the 6th string (low E) on your guitar. The top line represents the 1st string (high E).

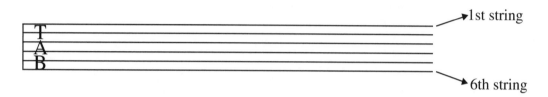

We use numbers representing the frets on the fretboard to show where your fingers should be placed. Read from left to right, placing your fingers on the frets indicated.

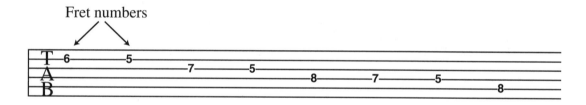

Chords are shown this way:

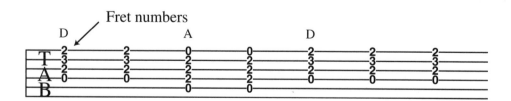

0 = Open string

hen necessary, your left-hand finger numbers (0 for open strings, 1, 2, 3 and 4) are shown
neath the lowest line.

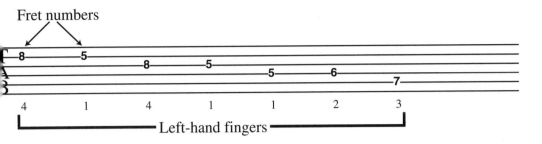

rmally, you will see standard music notation above the TAB. This is necessary for two rea-
ns. First—if you are reading the standard music notation and need additional clarification,
king down at the TAB can be of some help. Secondly, the notation will show you the rhythm
hole notes, half notes, quarter notes, etc.) of the fingerings you are reading from the TAB. It is
mmon for TAB to show frets only, without indicating the rhythm. In this case, the standard
sic notation above will tell you what you need to know.

ter in this book (page 51), you will learn the basics of reading standard notion.

New Strumming Rhythms

Earlier in this book (pages 18–21), you learned about whole notes, half notes, quarter notes, eighth notes and dotted half notes. A quick review is shown here:

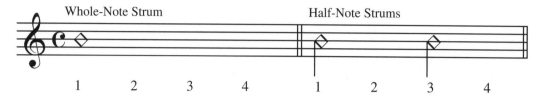

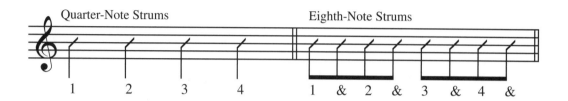

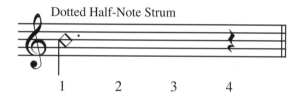

Let's add another strumming value to your arsenal.

The Sixteenth-Note Strum

Remember that when playing eighth notes we strum once (usually a downstroke) on the onbeat and once (usually an upstroke) on the offbeat. *Sixteenth notes* are twice as fast as eighth notes. This means that we strum twice on the onbeat and twice on the offbeat. You may be wondering how you can divide a single beat into four equal parts. It's really pretty simple.

When we play eighth notes the beat number is always the onbeat. We usually use the word "and" (or "&") for the offbeats. This divides the beat into two equal parts.

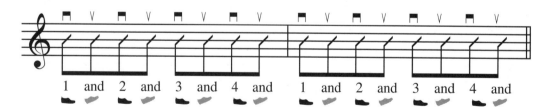

play sixteenth notes, we play two notes on the onbeat and two notes on the offbeat. The beat number is still on the onbeat and the "and" is still used for the offbeat, but now we have two new syllables—the "e" and the "a"—which fall after the onbeat and offbeat, respectively.

Sixteenth-Note Strums

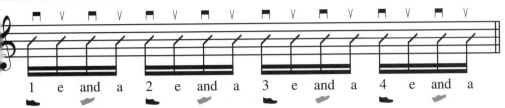

Practice the following sixteenth-note strums.

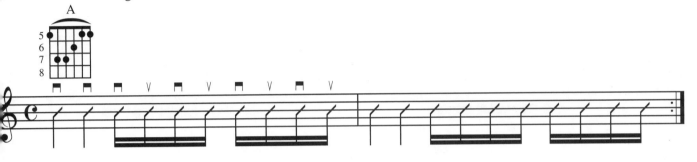

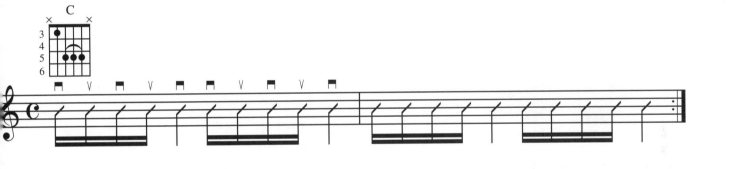

Remember this guy?
***Jimi Hendrix** (1942–1970) is
one of the main reasons
many of us picked up the
guitar in the first place.*

PHOTO • CORTESY OF STAR FILES, INC.

Part 2: Chords **37**

Here are more strumming patterns with sixteenth notes to practice.

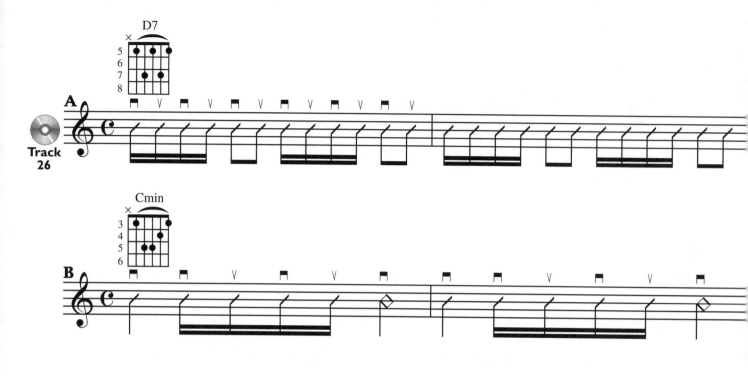

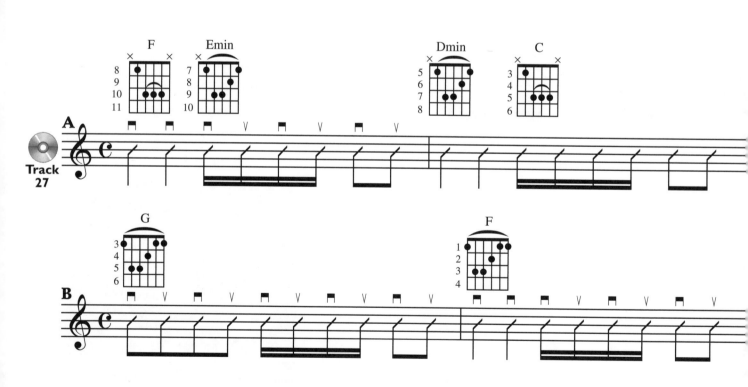

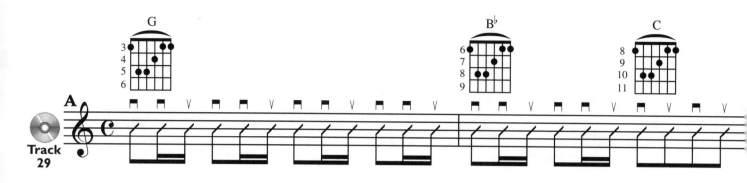

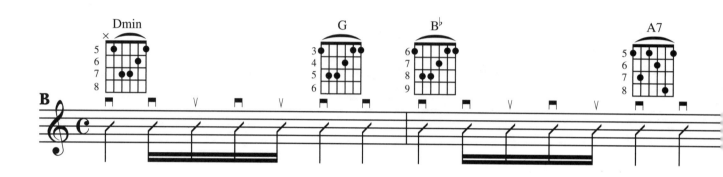

The Dotted Eighth-Note Strum

Even if the dotted eighth-note strum looks new and complicated to you, rest assured, you are very familiar with its sound. As you know, a dot increases a note's value by half (page 19). The half-note strum gets two beats; the dotted half note strum gets three beats (2 + 1 = 3). When an eighth-note strum—which is equal to two sixteenth-note strums—is dotted, it becomes equal to three sixteenth-note strums.

When followed by a sixteenth note, the dotted eighth-note strum is held for the duration of "1–e–and" and the sixteenth note falls on the "a." This rhythm uses the same amount of time as two eighth notes but has a more "swinging" effect.

Dotted Eighth-/Sixteenth-Note Strum

1   e   and   a

As always, rhythms are better understood when heard, so be sure to listen to the examples on the CD included with this book.

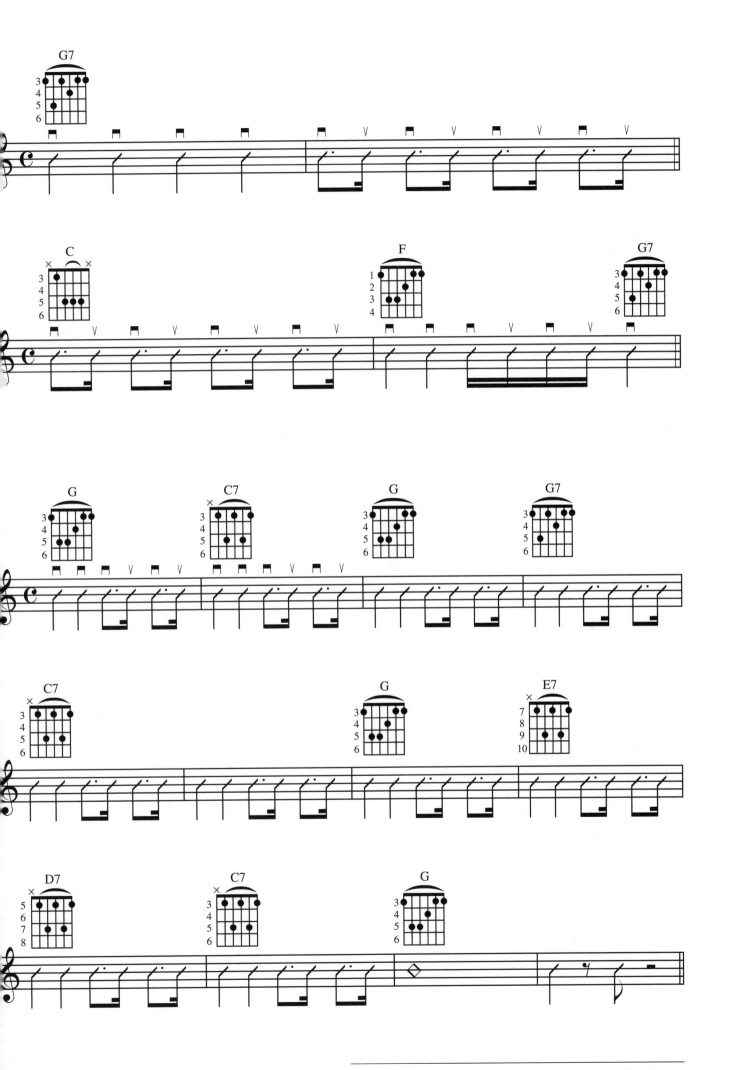

New Chords and Techniques

Now is a good time to add a few more chords to your vocabulary. The following *9* chords were used in many styles of music you listened to growing up. Like the 7 chords, 9 chords fall into the dominant family. You can often use them as substitutes for your dominant 7 chords. In other words, try using a D9 chord instead of a D7, or a G9 instead of a G7. It may not always be what you want, but it is fun to experiment this way.

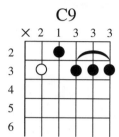

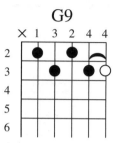

Lots of blues and rock-blues songs do not use full chords. These two-note chords are known as *5* or *power* chords and are often used instead of more traditional chords. Like barre chords, they take their root name from the notes on the 5th and 6th strings.

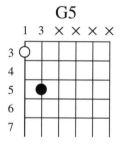

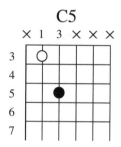

Chokes

Another new sign you will see in strum-rhythm notation is the "×." This signifies that the strum is executed on muted strings, creating an unpitched, percussive sound. To accomplish this, simply place your left-hand fingers over the strings just firmly enough to stop the strings from ringing and strum. This "clicking" sound is sometimes called a *choke* or a *chuck*. Once again, the CD included with this book should help clarify this technique.

× = Choke. Strum the muted strings.

e many examples that follow are common rhythms found in blues, rock and many other
les of popular music. Try to memorize the ones you really enjoy so that you can apply them
the songs you are learning at any time.

uesy Progressions

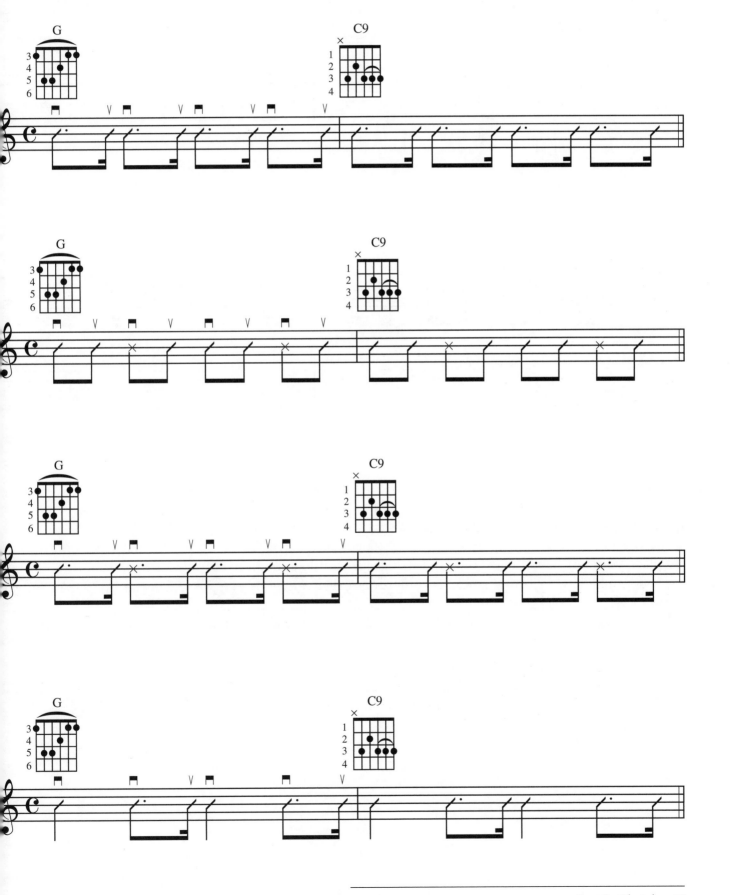

The following blues examples are typical blues rhythm guitar patterns that are a little more involved than simply strumming chords. The power chord is used and then a finger is added on the higher of the two strings, creating what is often called a *blues shuffle pattern*. You'll recognize it right away! Reading TAB was covered on pages 34 and 35.

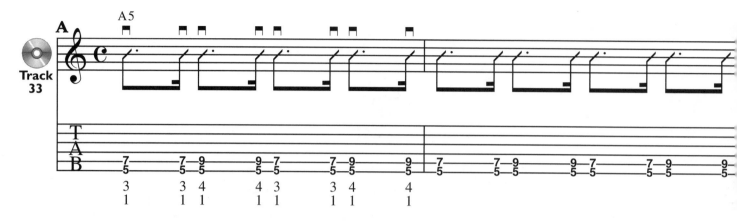

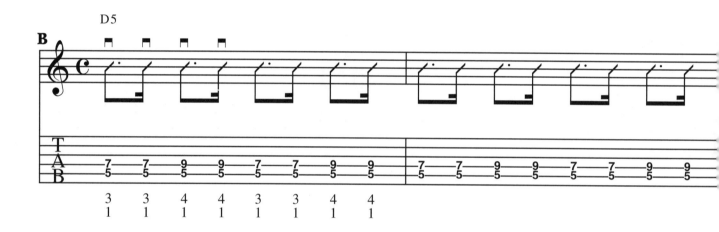

Some variations on this pattern involve stretching the 4th finger a bit further. Again, you'll recognize the sound. If the stretch feels difficult, don't practice till it hurts, which could cause injury. Over time, it will get easier if you're careful not to overdo it.

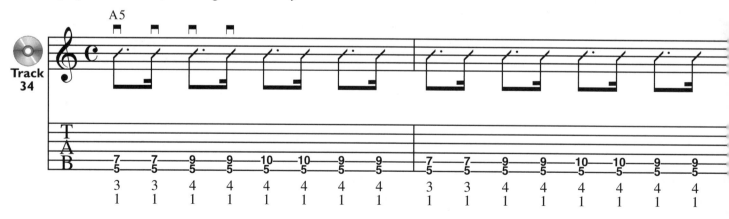

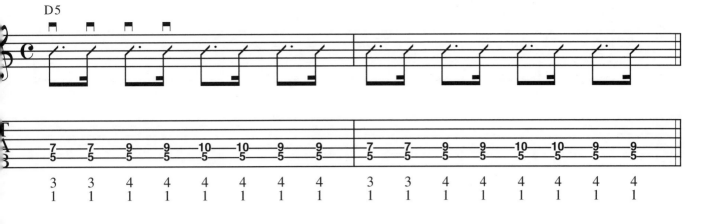

her variations include single notes.

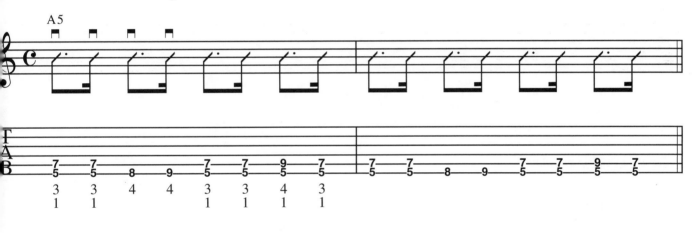

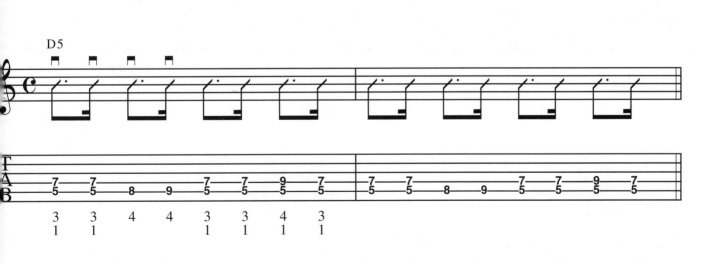

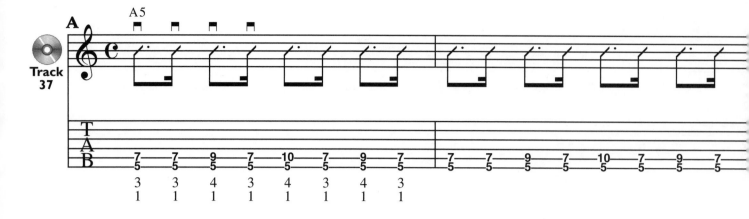

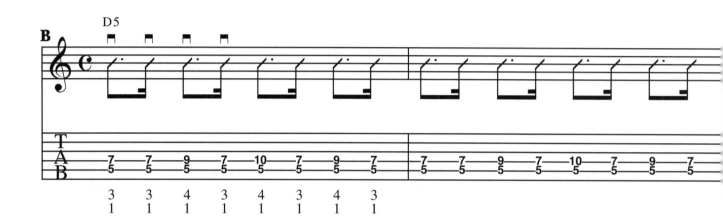

Rock Progressions

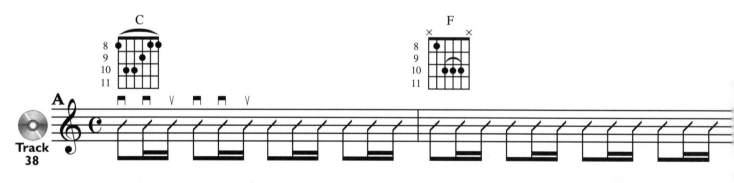

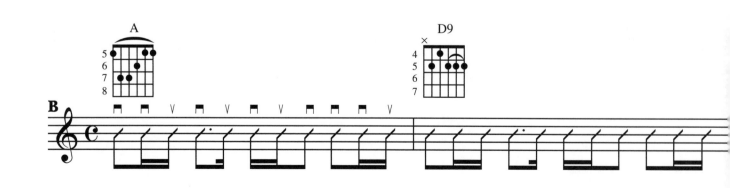

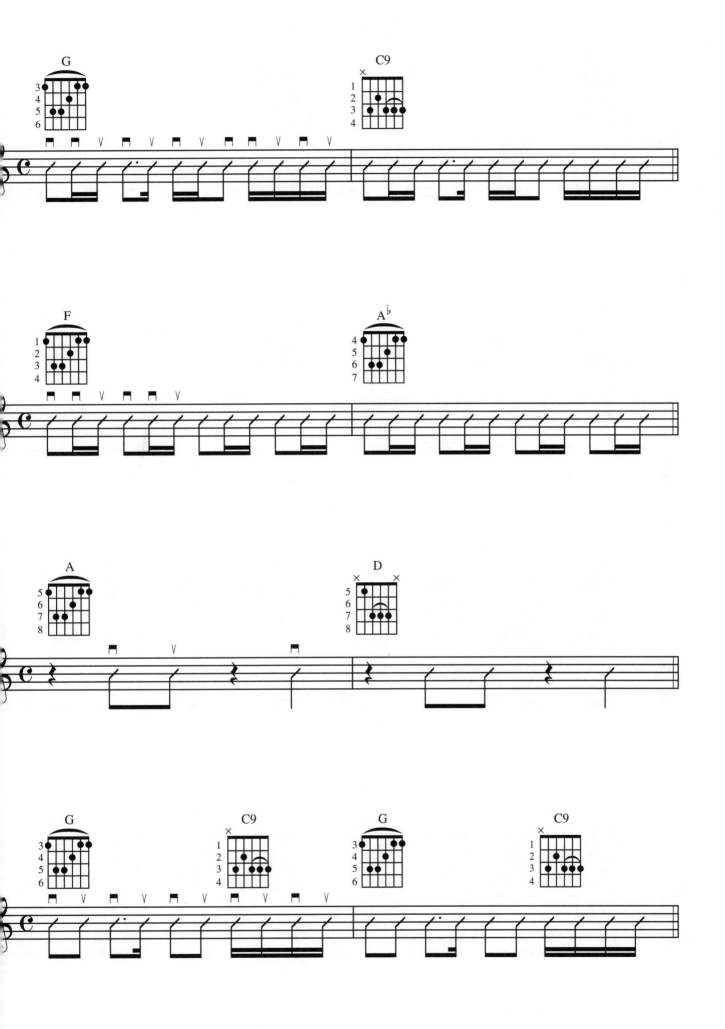

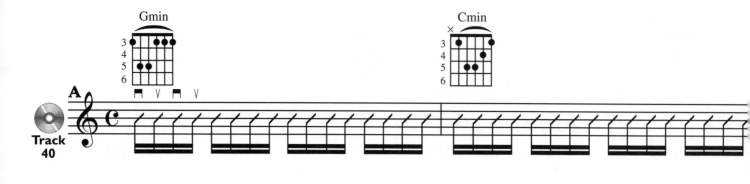

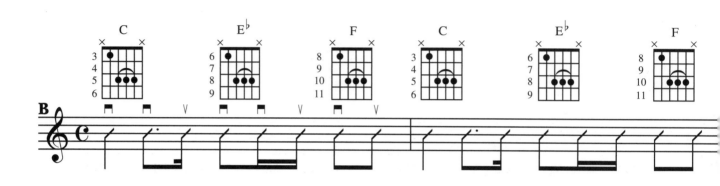

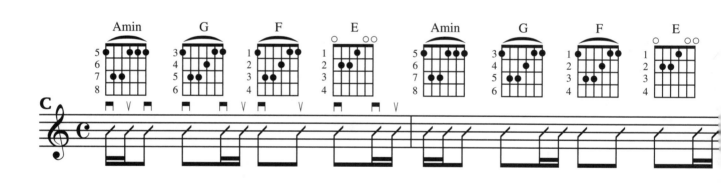

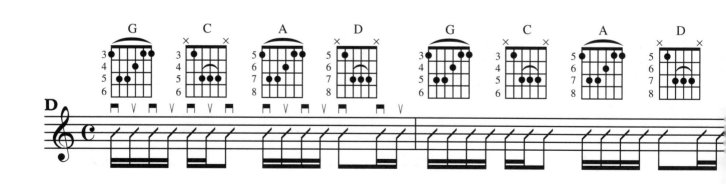

unky Stuff

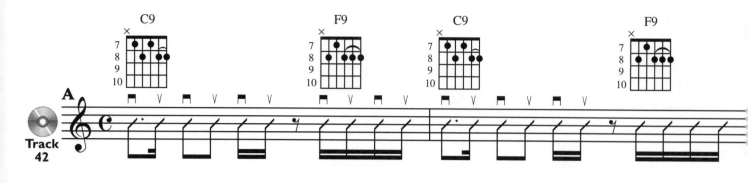

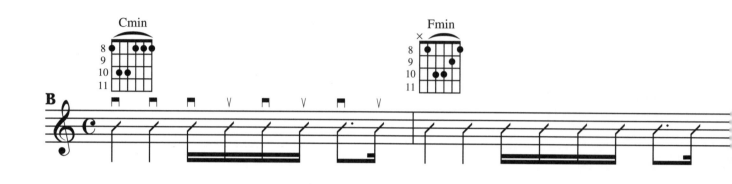

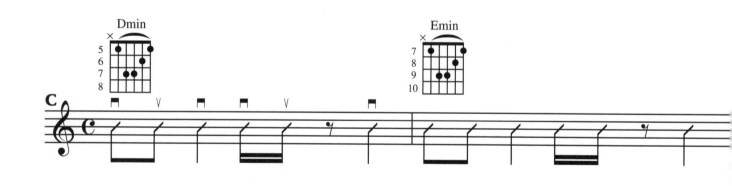

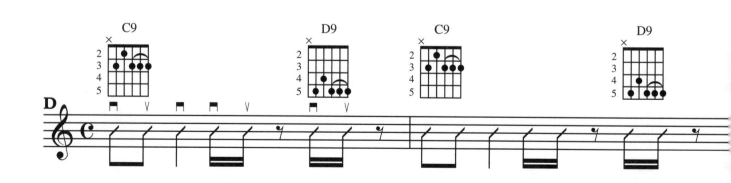

Part 3: Reading Standard Music Notation

some guitar players, learning to read music sounds like a scary, mysterious and painful ocess—but it really isn't. Since so many players start out learning a few chords that enable m to play songs and have a good time, learning to read standard music notation just doesn't m to be a priority. But acquiring this skill will help you learn songs faster, help you to ter understand some of the things you are playing and give you the ability to communicate th other musicians on a more advanced level. We're not talking about becoming an ace ht-reader here—just the ability to decipher enough printed music to suit your needs. This apter will show you some fundamentals and get you started reading music within the first four ts of the guitar, sometimes referred to as *1st position*.

tch

e Staff and Clef

uitar music is written on a series of five lines and four spaces called a *staff*. Additional lines and aces are created by adding lines above and below the staff called *ledger lines*.

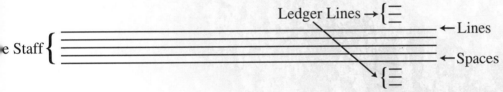

usic is a language, and like any other language, it has an alphabet, which contains seven letters at are repeated again and again: A–B–C–D–E–F–G–A–B–C–D–E–F–G. Each letter in the habet represents a specific *pitch* (degree of highness or lowness of a musical sound).

clef is placed at the beginning of the staff. Guitarists read the *G clef*. The line that its tail circles is given the name G. When the G clef encircles the second line, it is called the *treble* f. Knowing that the second line is G enables us to determine the names of all the lines and aces by simply going forward (up) or back (down) through the alphabet. This process can then continued for the ledger lines, should they appear.

elpful Hint—You can easily memorize the names of the lines and spaces by using the phrase very **G**ood **B**oy **D**oes **F**ine" for the lines and by observing that the spaces spell the word ACE."

(Treble) clef

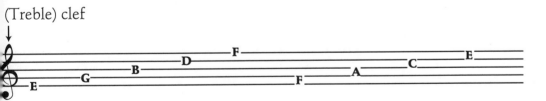

otes are placed on the staff showing which pitch to play. A note inherits the name of the line or ace on which it sits.

Notes

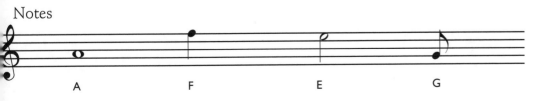

Every note on (or above or below) the staff corresponds to a note on the guitar. In more advanced levels of reading, we find that the same note can appear many times on the fretboard, but you don't have to worry about this right now. Reading in the 1st position has only one duplicated note that you'll find out about soon.

One good reason to learn to read standard music notation is that, by looking at a piece of printed music, you can start to see the contour of the melody. The higher pitched notes are in the upper regions of the staff. Lower notes reside lower in the staff. In this way, written music is truly representative of the way music sounds.

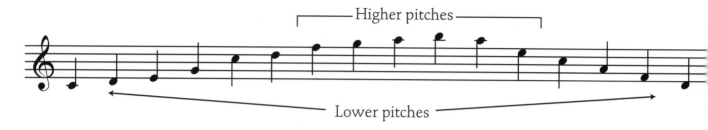

Time

It is not enough to simply know the notes on the staff and where they lie on the fretboard. Music is an art form that happens in time—it starts at one point in time and ends later on. We have to know how long to let one note or chord ring before striking the next. Sometimes there are periods of silence to keep track of as well.

Beats and Measures

When we play music, it is up to us to set the *tempo* (speed) of a song. Once this is set, we—along with our listeners—feel this beat and often keep track of the time by tapping our foot. We do this because we are feeling the *rhythmic pulse*, which we measure in *beats*. As you tap your foot, each tap on the floor is another beat.

Written music is divided into groups of beats called *measures*, which are marked with *bar lines*. A *double bar* is used to show the end of a short example or section.

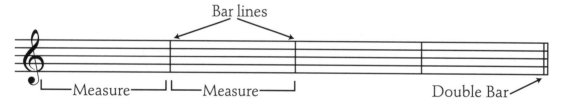

Note and Rest Values

The appearance of a note tells us how long a note is supposed to ring. The longest note is a *whole note*. A *half note* is half as long as a whole note. A *quarter note* is half as long as a half note and an *eighth note* is half as long as a quarter note.

These note values relate directly to the strumming values you have already learned in this book.

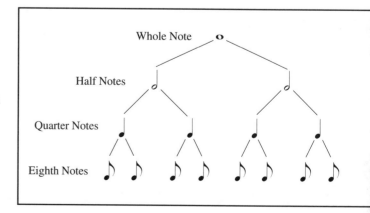

same values exist for rests.

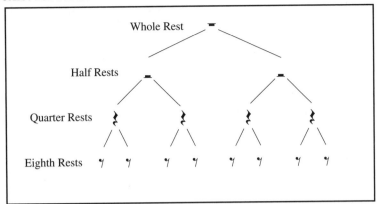

e Time Signature

u will see two numbers at the beginning of every piece of music. This is the *time signature* d it tells us how to count the beats. The top number tells us how many beats there will be in th measure. If there is a **4** on top, we know there will be four beats in every measure, which 1 include any combination of notes and rests that equal four beats when added together.

e bottom number tells us which kind of note will receive one beat. A **4** on the bottom means at the quarter note gets one beat.

4 = Four beats per measure
4 = The quarter note ♩ gets one beat

llowing are the note values in $\frac{4}{4}$, which is so common it is also known as *common time* adicated with a **C**).

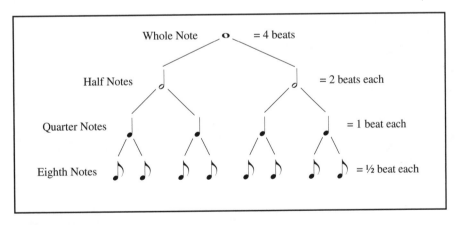

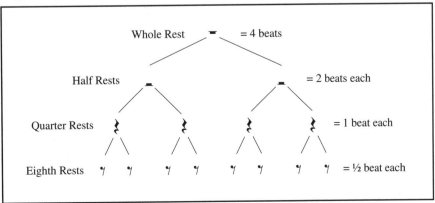

Beams

When eighth notes appear consecutively, they are *beamed* together, as with eighth-note strums. They are also counted the same way as eighth-note strums.

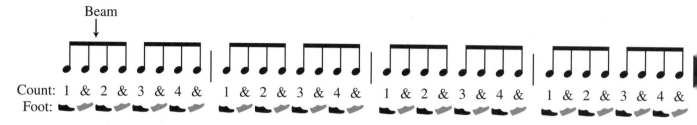

Another Time Signature

Another common time signature you need to know is $\frac{3}{4}$.

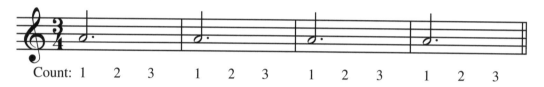

3 = Three beats per measure
4 = The quarter note ♩ gets one beat

Dotted Notes

As with strumming values, a dot increases a note's value by half. A *dotted half note* gets three beats.

Rhythm Exercises

Using the open 1st string, practice the rhythm exercises below. Be sure to tap your foot to help you keep track of the time.

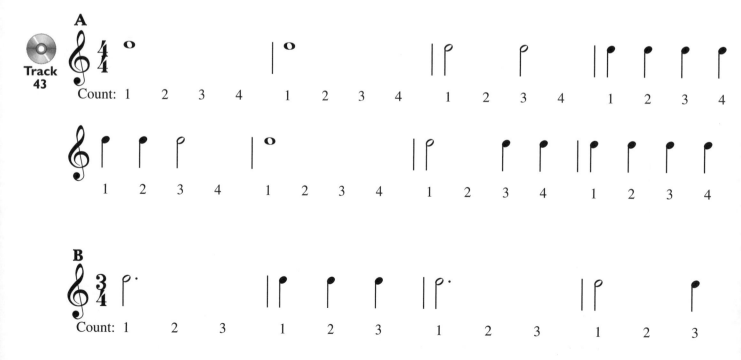

Notes on the 6th (Low E) String

Below are the first five notes on the 6th string. As we briefly discussed on page 25, the sharp ♯ raises a note one fret and the flat ♭ lowers a note one fret. You will find sharps and flats between all notes except B and C and E and F. Also remember that any sharp can be spelled as a flat, and vice versa. For example F♯ can be spelled G♭. These are called enharmonic equivalents.

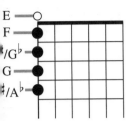

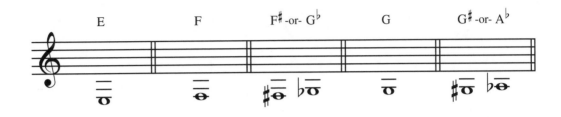

Practice this until it feels easy.

Count: 1 2 3 4   1 2 3 4   1 2 3 4   1 2 3 4

1 2 3 4   1 2 3 4   1 2 3 4   1 2 3 4

Notes on the 5th (A) String

Here are the first five notes on the 5th string.

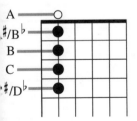

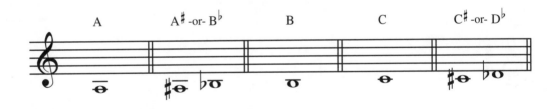

Practice this exercise on the 5th string.

Count: 1 2 3 4   1 2 3 4   1 2 3 4   1 2 3 4

1 2 3 4   1 2 3 4   1 2 3 4   1 2 3 4

Since an accidental is only in effect for the measure in which it appears, these notes are not sharped.

Part 3: Reading Standard Music Notation 55

This exercise combines notes on the 5th and 6th strings.

Notes on the 4th (D) String

Here are the first five notes on the 4th string.

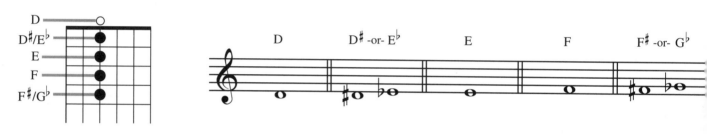

Exercise on the 4th string.

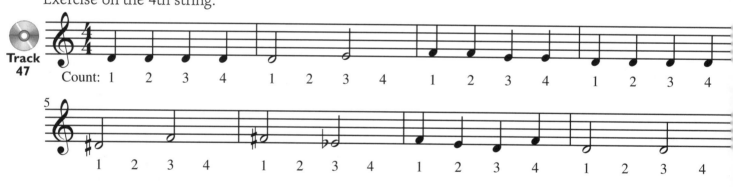

Combining notes on the 4th, 5th and 6th strings.

Notes on the 3rd (G) String

Here are the first five notes on the 3rd string.

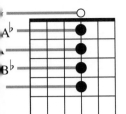

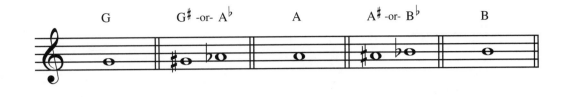

Exercise on the 3rd string.

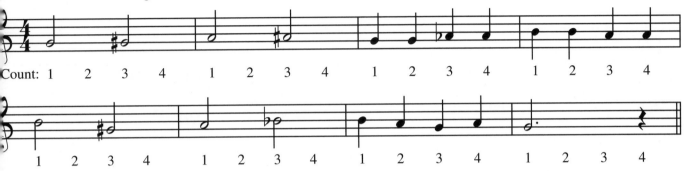

Combining notes on the 3rd, 4th, 5th and 6th strings.

Notes on the 2nd (B) String

Here are the first five notes on the 2nd string.

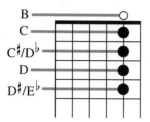
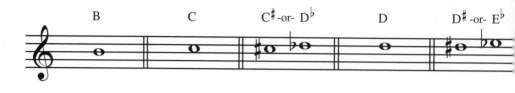

Exercise on the 2nd string.

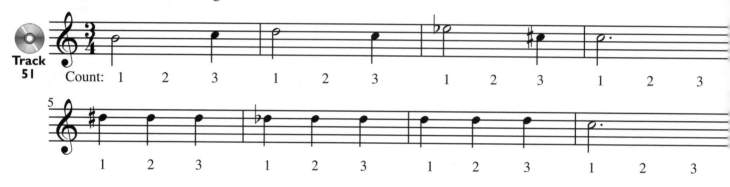

Combining notes on the 2nd, 3rd, 4th, 5th and 6th strings.

otes on the 1st (High E) String

:re are the first five notes on the 1st string.

:rcise on the 1st string.

Count: 1 2 3 4   1 2 3 4   1 2 3 4   1 2 3 4

1 2 3 4   1 2 3 4   1 2 3 4   1 2 3 4

ombining notes on all six strings.

Count: 1 2 3 4   1 2 3 4   1 2 3 4   1 2 3 4

1 2 3 4   1 2 3 4   1 2 3 4   1 2 3 4

1 2 3 4   1 2 3 4   1 2 3 4   1 2 3 4

1 2 3 4   1 2 3 4   1 2 3 4   1 2 3 4

1 2 3 4   1 2 3 4   1 2 3 4   1 2 3 4

1 2 3 4   1 2 3 4   1 2 3 4   1 2 3 4

here is much more to know, but now you have an idea of what is involved and the ability to owly pick out melodies in songbooks or sheet music.

Now that you can read standard music notation, let's do something altogether different from the strumming we have covered thus far. Using the very common marriage of standard music notation with TAB, we'll take a brief look at the huge guitar topic of fingerpicking!

Fingerpicking

The term *fingerpicking* refers to sounding the strings with the fingers of your right hand instead of a pick. You have heard this technique in all styles of music from folk, rock and country all the way to jazz.

Since there are hundreds of different fingerpicking patterns, the examples that follow are intended to get you started in this style or possibly just reacquaint you with some things you've done before.

As you know, we identify our fretting fingers with the numbers 1, 2, 3 and 4. We use letters to designate the fingers of our picking hand.

> *p* = thumb
> *i* = first finger
> *m*= middle finger
> *a* = ring finger

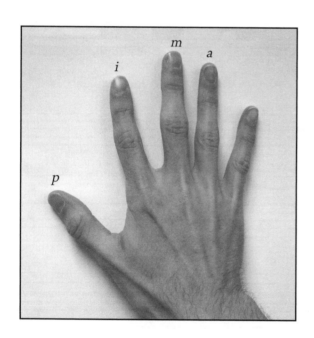

Take a look at the examples on page 61 (the facing page). You will see these letters in the standard music notation, telling you which right-hand finger to use for each note.

Your hand and wrist placement is important when fingerpicking. For now, just try to remember to keep your wrist rather high above the guitar so that your fingers dangle into the strings below. Swing your fingers back toward the bridge of your guitar to create some distance between *p* and *i*.

As a starting point, assign *p* to the bass strings and let *i*, *m* and *a* take care of the 3rd, 2nd and 1st strings, respectively. These finger/string assignments are not carved in stone; in reality, you may move them around quite a bit, but this is a good way to start learning some simple patterns.

As always, work slowly and patiently, trying to maintain a steady rhythm and even tone.

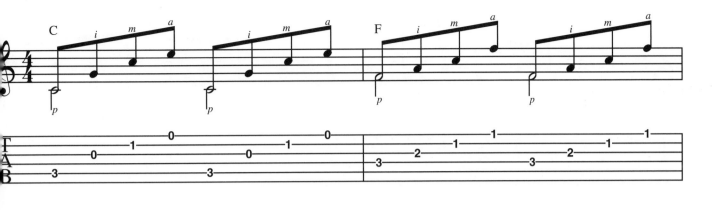

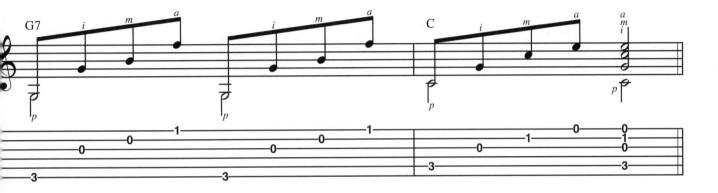

his example has a *key signature*. A key signature shows the notes that will be played sharp or
t (never both) in a piece of music. In this case, all F- or C-notes are played as sharps (F♯ and C♯).
his is called the *key of D Major*.

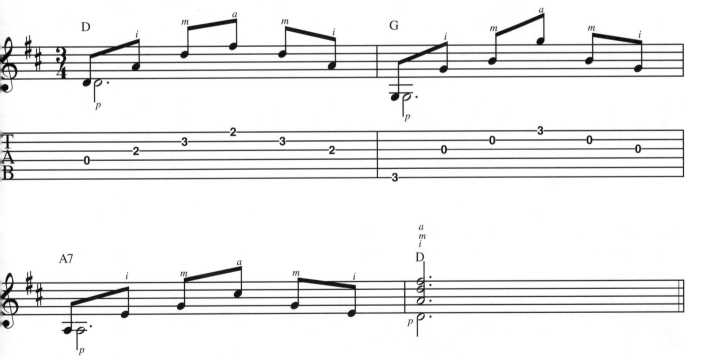

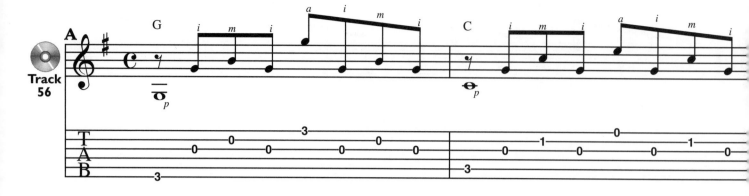

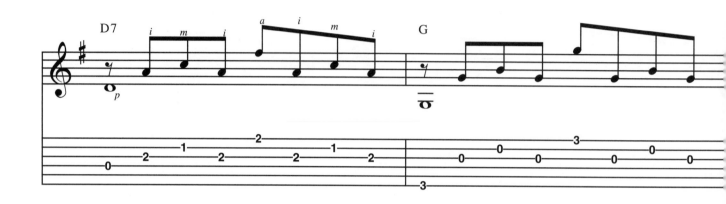

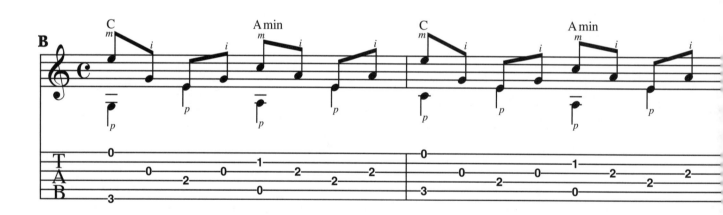

Notice this next example uses *ties*. A tie is a curved line that connects two notes of the same pitch. The second note in a tie is not struck; rather, its value is added to that of the first. In other words, the first note is held for the time of both notes. In the TAB, a tied note is shown in parentheses.

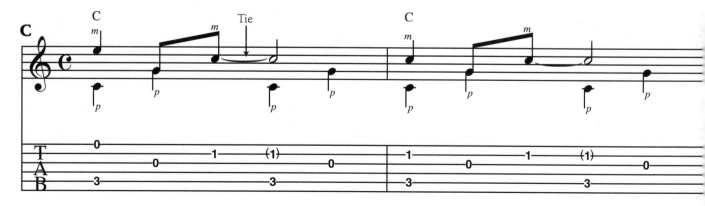

Part 4: Improvising

If you have ever played in a band, you probably remember that one of the most enjoyable aspects was improvising or "playing lead." This was your chance to shine, an opportunity to play your own thing extemporaneously and create some excitement within the song. For you, the following chapters will contain information you may have once known along with loads of new ideas to help you pick up wherever you left off on the road to becoming a great lead player; whether you play rock, blues, folk or any other pop style.

If you didn't play lead guitar in your earlier guitar-playing days but always found it intriguing, this section will be the perfect place for you to begin. We'll start with very basic information and continue on to more involved concepts.

Band or No Band

Except for some very advanced styles of solo guitar, improvising generally assumes that you are playing with other people. In most cases, there is a section in most songs where the vocal ends and an instrumental improvisation begins. There can be a specified amount of time for this to happen, or sometimes the improvised solo is open-ended. In either case, the vocal usually comes back in afterwards and the song ends sometime later.

Most improvised solos are constructed with single notes. The rest of the band provides the accompaniment—they play the chords and keep the rhythm going. A first, very important step in learning to improvise is learning what notes sound good over all the various chords.

Getting together with other players even once in a while can go a long way in learning to improvise. This is the way to find out if you are making progress in your practicing. Even if you don't have the opportunity to practice with others, it is still possible to make headway in your improvising. Here are some other options:

1. There are many play-along book and CD sets you can purchase. Basically, you play along with a "backup" band that is recorded on the CD. The book shows you the chord progression, some improvisational tools and a basic outline of the arrangement for you to work with. These are available in all styles and levels. Check out the *Stand-Alone* series from the National Guitar Workshop and Alfred. Plus, you'll find a few tracks to practice with on the CD included with this book.

2. There are also many computer programs available to work with. These range in complexity from very simple to very complicated depending on the level of interactivity. One of the cool aspects of this option is that you can usually speed up or slow down the tempos to suit your level of ability.

3. You can also accomplish quite a bit by recording chord progressions yourself. These will enable you to construct whole arrangements of songs as well as providing you with a way to practice your improvising.

While all of these methods are good, remember that there really is no substitute for playing with other people. Acting and reacting to what others are playing has a lot to do with the art of improvising.

provising with Scales—The Pentatonic Scale

haps the simplest way to begin improvising is with *scales*. A scale is a series a notes arranged habetically in a specific order of whole steps (a distance of two frets) and half steps (one fret). st folks start with scales because you can sound pretty good right away. Most popular music kes use of the *pentatonic* scales. These are five-note scales that come in two flavors—major minor—and are heard frequently in rock and blues.

e best thing about the pentatonic scales is that they can be used easily in many situations. In er words, one can often play the notes in these scales pretty freely over an entire chord prossion. You still have to know which scale to use for any given chord progression, but once ı know that, it's difficult to make "mistakes."

e Minor Pentatonic Scale

e *minor pentatonic* scale is one of the most popular scales used to improvise over rock and es songs. Take a look at the following scale fingering. It is a G Minor Pentatonic scale; notice t the first note—called the *tonic*—is a G on the 6th string. This is a *closed* fingering, so—like re chords—you can move this fingering all over the neck to other tonics. To demonstrate this nt, the A Minor, C Minor and E Minor Pentatonic scales are also shown below.

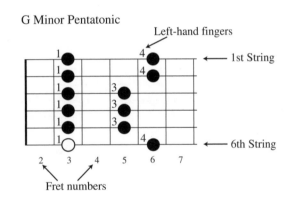

G Minor Pentatonic

Left-hand fingers

← 1st String

← 6th String

Fret numbers

○ = Tonic. First note and namesake of the scale.

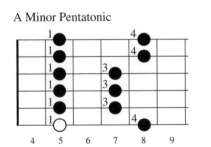

A Minor Pentatonic

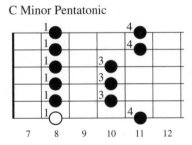

C Minor Pentatonic

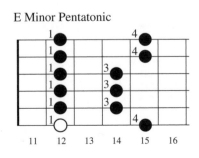

E Minor Pentatonic

In order to start improvising, we need a chord progression over which to play. We'll start by improvising over blues progressions.

A blues progression is a 12-bar chord progression repeated over and over. You played through some blues progressions in Part 2 of this book (for example, pages 14–16). This is a perfect place to start because you can improvise using a single minor pentatonic scale over the entire progression.

To determine which scale to play, simply match the key of the blues progression with the tonic of the minor pentatonic scale. The blues progression shown here is in the key of "G." We know this because the first chord is a G, and a 12-bar blues starts on a chord with the same name as the key. When it's time to start improvising, you will use the G Minor Pentatonic scale, shown again below for your convenience.

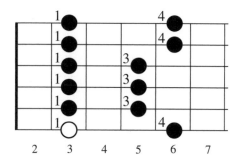

ow to Get Started Improvising

re is a procedure to follow to get started improvising.

Step 1: Become familiar with the sound of the progression. Learn to play the whole progression with the chords shown. Use the chord shapes you learned in Part 2 of this book.

Step 2: Record this progression. This progression is also found on the CD included with this book so you can choose to play along with that instead.

Step 3: Improvise! Start by simply playing the scale up and down to see how the various notes sound against the chords.

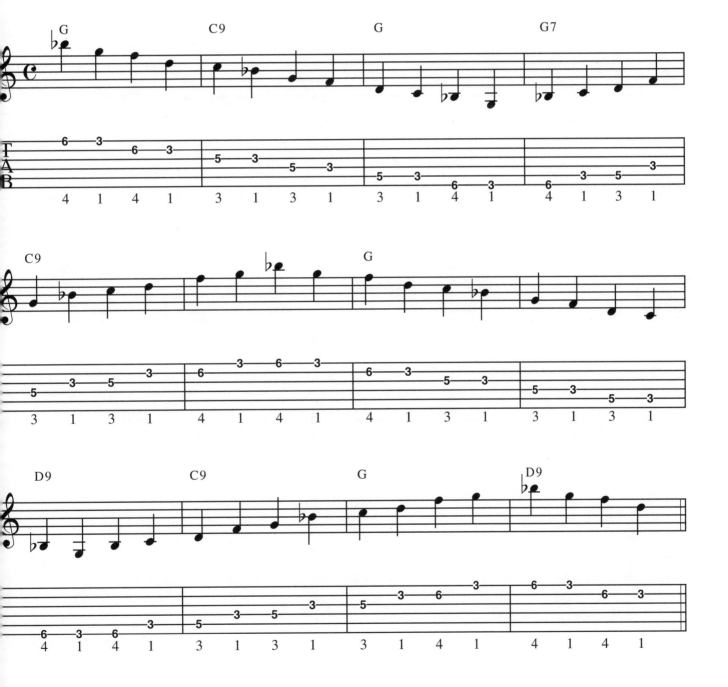

Then try playing the notes in random order.

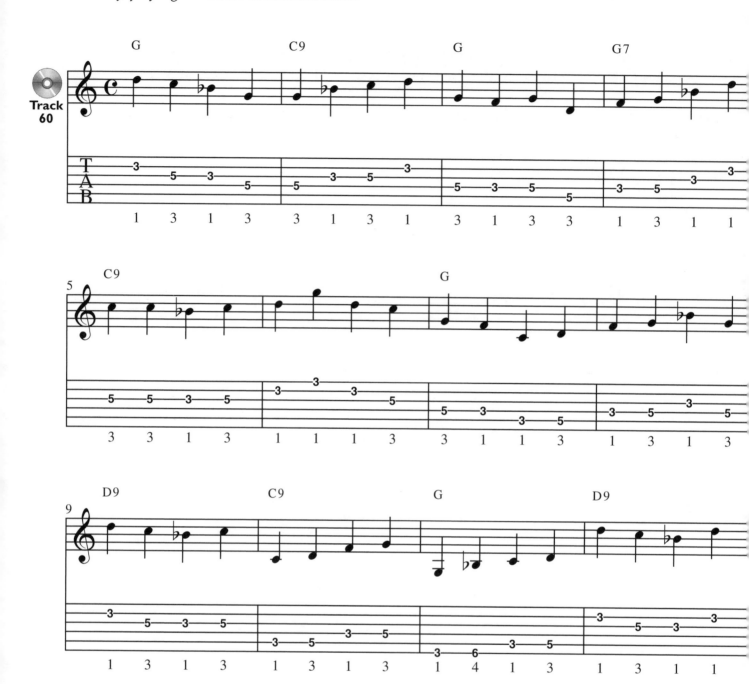

ow, try varying the rhythms of the notes.

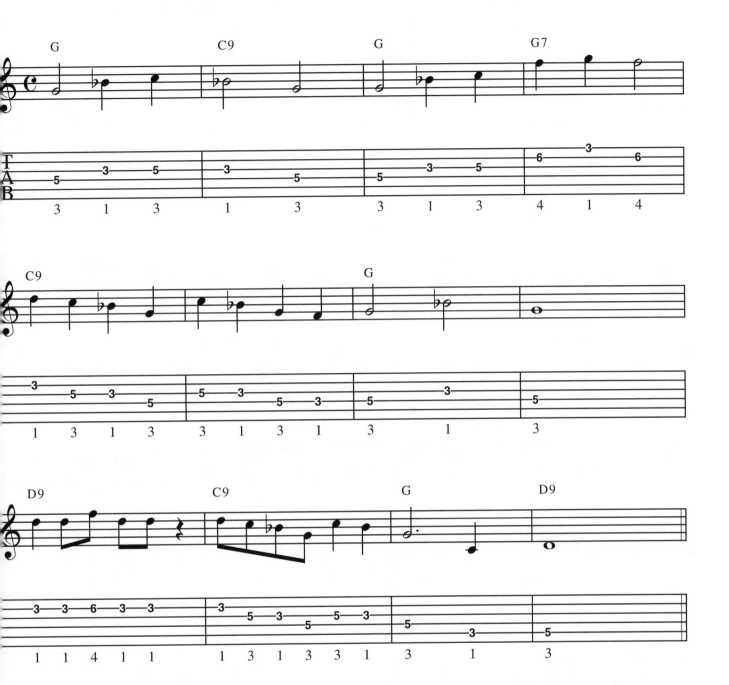

Here are a number of short solos for you to play. They incorporate the various note values you have learned. When you feel comfortable with these, practice playing along with the progression on the CD (use your balance control to "dial out" the lead guitar) and come up with your own ideas.

Improvising in Various Keys

Let's start moving both the chord progression and the scale around a little.
The progressions are shown with a few variations. Don't worry, the scale
will still sound good. Simply use these variations to help you expand your
chord vocabulary a little. At right is the scale for this blues in A.

A Minor Pentatonic

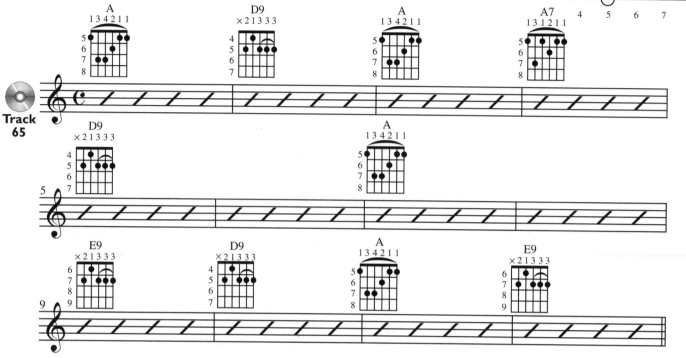

Here is the scale for the following blues in C.

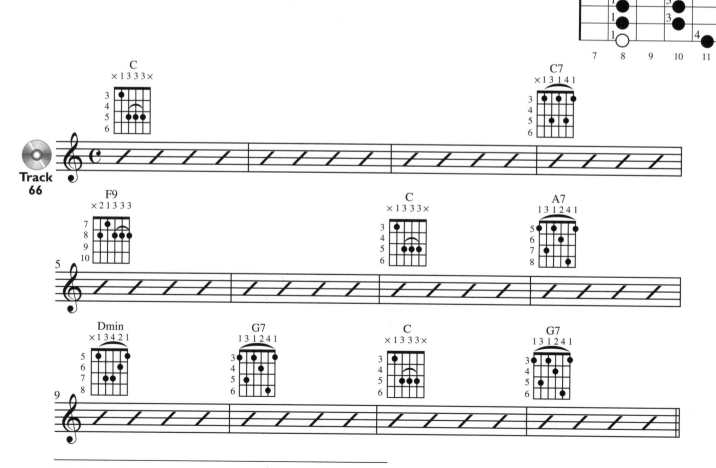

C Minor Pentatonic

This is the scale to use for the following blues in E.

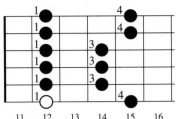

E Minor Pentatonic

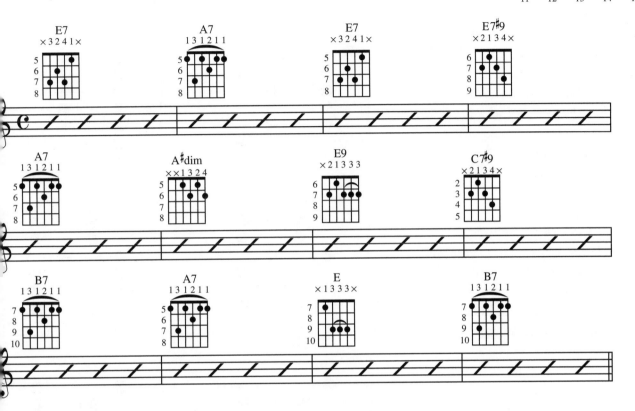

ditional Fingerings

now you should be starting to sound pretty good. It's time to learn the rest of the minor ntatonic scale fingerings. This will allow you to play over the same blues progressions using e entire range of the fretboard. The fingerings are shown for the G Minor Pentatonic scale. ter you have learned these, you need to become comfortable with moving them around to the her keys. It's really pretty easy, but it will take some time. Have fun—no pressure!

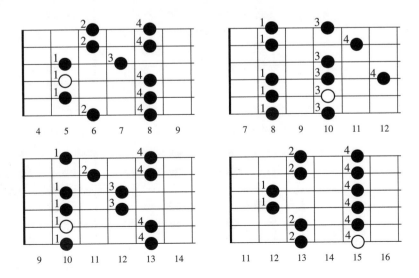

would be a very good idea to practice these new fingerings over the blues progressions shown these pages (72–73).

The Major Pentatonic Scale

Sometimes it seems like the amount of information there is to know about guitar playing is endless; and actually—it is. Occasionally, however, we run into a concept that gives us a lot of mileage without having to devote much time or effort. The pentatonic scales fall into this category because *the fingerings for both the major and minor pentatonic scales are identical.* Only the tonic's location within the fingerings change. The left column in the chart below shows the minor pentatonic scale fingerings you already know. Next to each one is the major pentatonic scale that shares the fingering. All you really have to do is note the new location of the tonic.

The major pentatonic is a happier-sounding pentatonic scale and is handy for improvising over blues progressions with major and dominant chords and in country or Southern rock (Poco, Lynard Skynard, etc.) contexts. This is not a good scale choice, however, for improvising over a blues with minor chords.

As with the minor pentatonic scale, simply match the key of the progression with the tonic of the major pentatonic scale. For example, if a blues progression starts with an A chord, use the A Major Pentatonic scale.

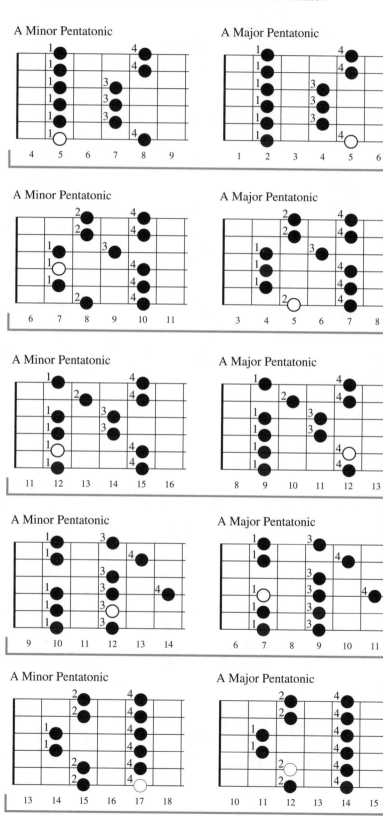

can use the major pentatonic scale in many of the same situations as the minor pentatonic.
ing this will give you two distinctively different types of sounds to create your solo ideas
m. Simply put, the minor pentatonic will give you a bluesier or more rock sound while the
jor pentatonic will add a sweeter, more country sound.

's organize this information so we can use it more easily. The major and minor pentatonic
les are related. Every major pentatonic scale can be coupled with a minor pentatonic scale and
en, depending on the style of music and the chord progression itself, can be used
erchangeably. There are many ways to explain this theoretically, but for our purposes the
iest way to remember the major and minor pentatonic scales that go together would be as
lows:

1. By moving any minor pentatonic scale fingerings *down* three frets, you find the related
   major pentatonic scale.

2. By moving any major pentatonic scale *up* three frets, you find the related minor pentatonic
   scale.

y improvising over the following blues progressions using both the major and minor penta-
nic scales shown. You can play along with the CD included with this book, or record the
ogressions yourself using any chord form you prefer (see Part 2 of this book).

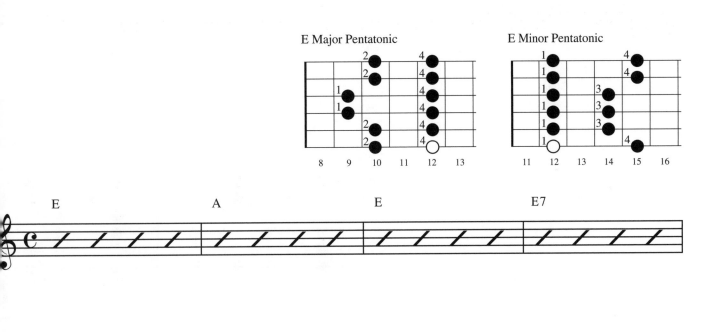

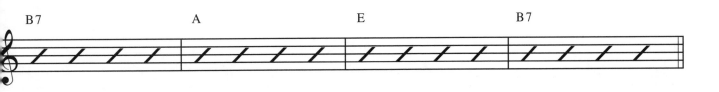

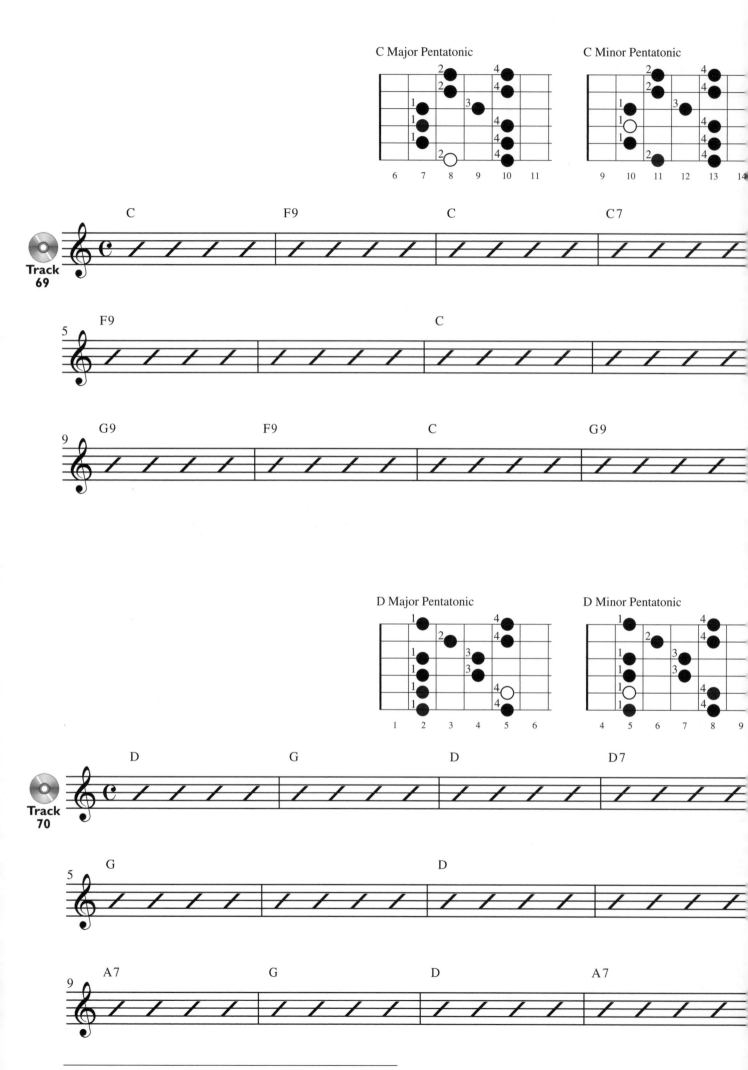

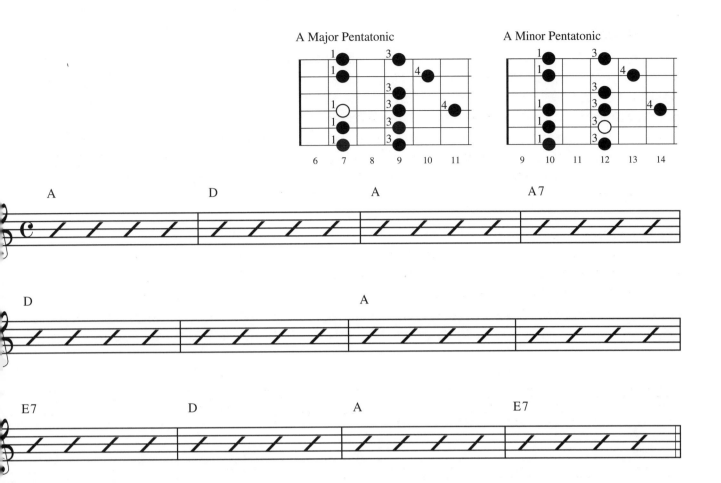

The Blues Scale

More good news! The *blues scale*, which will add a lot more excitement to your sound, is created by simply adding one note to the minor pentatonic scale fingerings you already know. The fingerings for the blues scales are shown below. Like the minor pentatonic scale, the tonic of the blues scale must match the key of the chord progression.

Blues Scale Fingerings

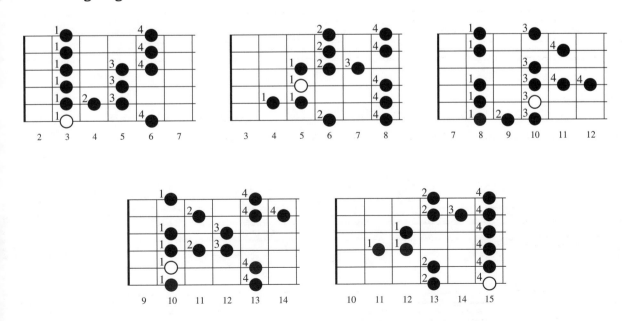

Now go back to all the progressions in this book and try using the blues scale in the place of the minor pentatonic scales you have been using. With these three scales, the minor pentatonic, major pentatonic and the blues scale, it is possible to recreate many of the sounds you hear in the music you listen to.

Basic Music Theory

Up to this point we have concentrated on the basics of rock and blues playing. Now, it's time to examine other kinds of chords and chord progressions and how to improvise in those situations. Rock and blues styles are very guitar-oriented. The sounds of barre chords and pentatonic scales practically define those styles. When we start playing styles of music that lie outside of those sounds, it is necessary to learn a little more about music theory and study the same topics as other instrumentalists. In other words, when playing rock and blues, it's fine to organize your knowledge from the point of view of the guitar fretboard; in other styles, we need to have a more universal view.

The Major Scale

Most of the chords we use can be understood in relation to the *major scale*. This is a collection of seven notes that musicians of all kinds have used for centuries. You have probably heard this scale countless times. Here is an example of a C Major scale over two *octaves* (the closest distance between any two notes with the same name). Playing the scale on a single string will help you become familiar with its structure. Play this and become familiar with its sound.

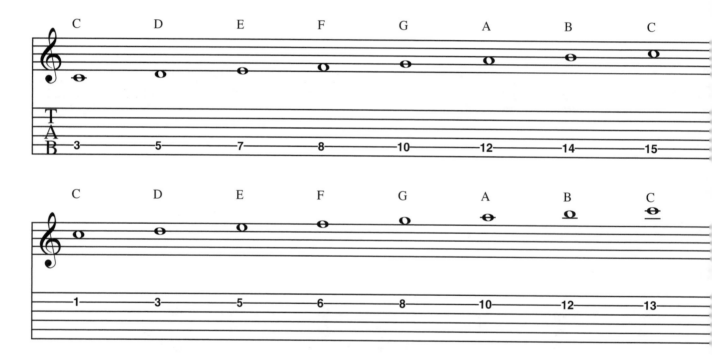

The Chromatic Scale

In the Western world we use a system of 12 notes called the *chromatic scale*. On the guitar it is found by simply playing consecutive notes, fret by fret along any single string.

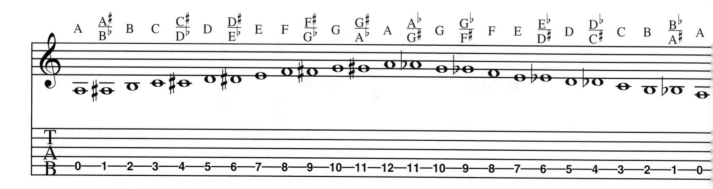

the chromatic scale, a move from any one note to the next is a half step (a distance of
 fret).

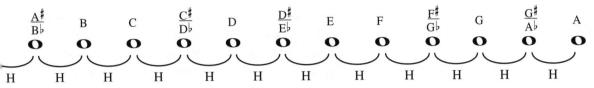

$$\begin{array}{cccccccccccc} \frac{A\#}{B\flat} & B & C & \frac{C\#}{D\flat} & D & \frac{D\#}{E\flat} & E & F & \frac{F\#}{G\flat} & G & \frac{G\#}{A\flat} & A \end{array}$$

⌣ / H = Half step

pping every other note (or fret) of the chromatic scale yields whole steps.

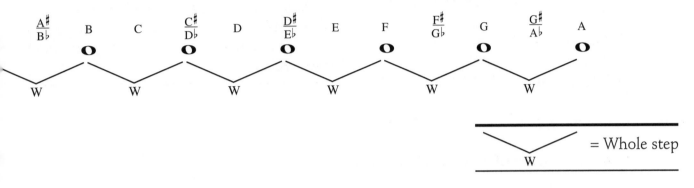

⌵ / W = Whole step

 can build major scales starting from any note in the chromatic scale using the following
mula:

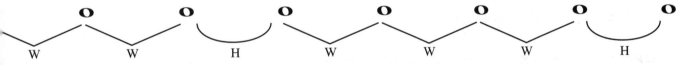

W   W   H   W   W   W   H

 a C Major scale would contain the following notes. Notice that the last note of a major scale
 always the same as the first.

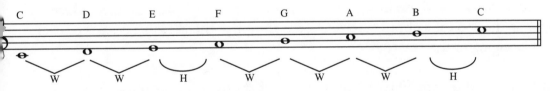

Major is the only major scale with no sharps or flats, because the half steps occur naturally
 tween E–F and B–C. For any other major scale, either flats or sharps (never both!) must be used
 make the notes fit the major scale formula. Here is the F Major scale.

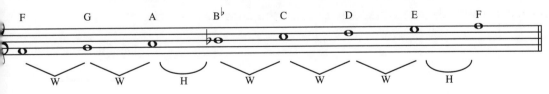

ere is the G Major scale.

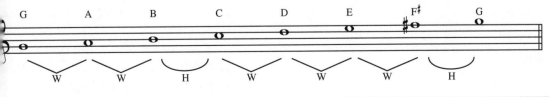

Keys

Here are the names of the notes in all the major scales.

C Major	C D E F G A B C
F Major	F G A B♭ C D E F
B♭ Major	B♭ C D E♭ F G A B♭
E♭ Major	E♭ F G A♭ B♭ C D E♭
A♭ Major	A♭ B♭ C D♭ E♭ F G A♭
D♭ Major	D♭ E♭ F G♭ A♭ B♭ C D♭
G♭ Major	G♭ A♭ B♭ C♭ D♭ E♭ F G♭
B Major	B C♯ D♯ E F♯ G♯ A♯ B
E Major	E F♯ G♯ A B C♯ D♯ E
A Major	A B C♯ D E F♯ G♯ A
D Major	D E F♯ G A B C♯ D
G Major	G A B C D E F♯ G

> The notes of a major scale also comprise the notes of a *key*. For example, the notes of a C Major scale comprise the key of C Major. On page 61 you learned about key signatures. A song with no sharps or flats in the key signature is in the key of C, because the C Major scale has no sharps or flats. The fingerpicking example on page 61 contained two sharps: F♯ and C♯. A piece with this key signature is in the key of D Major because the D Major scale contains these sharps.

While this may seem like a lot of information, you will find it necessary and not quite so hard to absorb over time. It is important because these scales are where all your chords come from.

The Theory Behind Chords

As you have just learned, songs are written in keys and every major scale corresponds to a key; Every note in each scale is the root of a chord. These chords comprise the *diatonic chords* of each key. Diatonic means "belonging to the key."

As you already know there are different "flavors" or qualities of chords, such as major, minor and dominant. There is a pattern of chord qualities that is the same in every major key. The pattern is shown below, using Roman numerals (this is a universal practice) to represent each of the seven different chords in the major scale (remember, the eighth note is the same as the first). This list contains one new chord quality: the *diminished* chord. A fingering for this chord is shown below on the right. This is a very unusual chord in that *any note in the chord can be the root*. Memorize this list.

I (1)   Major
II (2)   Minor
III (3)   Minor
IV (4)   Major
V (5)   Major
VI (6)   Minor
VII (7) Diminished

Diminished Chord

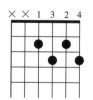

The chord symbol for a diminished chord is either "dim" or "○." In this book, we will use "dim."

e diatonic chords for C Major are as follows.

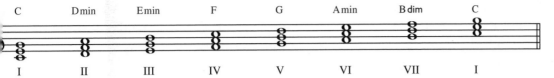

re are the diatonic chords for F Major.

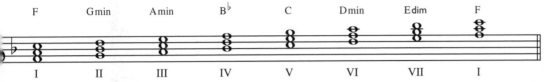

re are the diatonic chords for G Major.

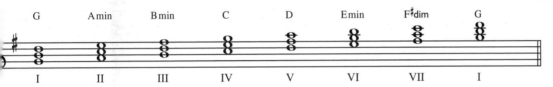

re is a reference chart that shows the diatonic chords for all 12 keys.

KEY   DIATONIC CHORDS

C	C	Dmin	Emin	F	G	Amin	Bdim
F	F	Gmin	Amin	B♭	C	Dmin	Edim
B♭	B♭	Cmin	Dmin	E♭	F	Gmin	Adim
E♭	E♭	Fmin	Gmin	A♭	B♭	Cmin	Ddim
A♭	A♭	B♭min	Cmin	D♭	E♭	Fmin	Gdim
D♭	D♭	E♭min	Fmin	G♭	A♭	B♭min	Cdim
G♭	G♭	A♭min	B♭min	C♭	D♭	E♭min	Fdim
B	B	C#min	D#min	E	F#	G#min	A#dim
E	E	F#min	G#min	A	B	C#min	D#dim
A	A	Bmin	C#min	D	E	F#min	G#dim
D	D	Emin	F#min	G	A	Bmin	C#dim
G	G	Amin	Bmin	C	D	Emin	F#dim

Diatonic Progressions

It is important to know the chords of the keys in which you play. You will find that many songs follow similar patterns. For example, notice the frequency with which II–V–I appears; it is one of the most commonly used chord progressions. Becoming familiar with how all of this is organized should help you learn—or even compose—songs much more quickly.

Here are a few sample progressions using diatonic chords. Practice them to become familiar with the sound. The chord fingerings shown are suggestions; you can use any chord fingering you prefer.

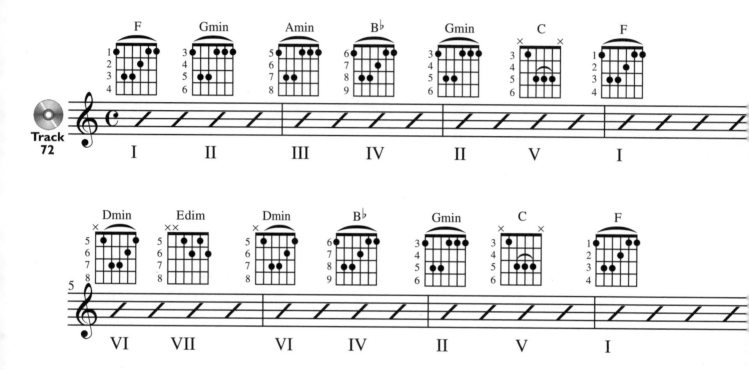

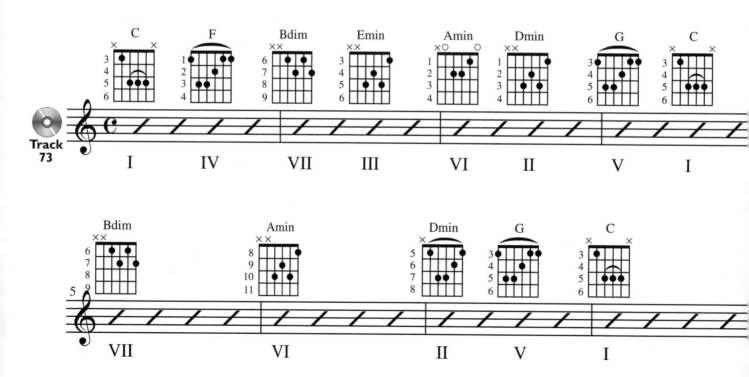

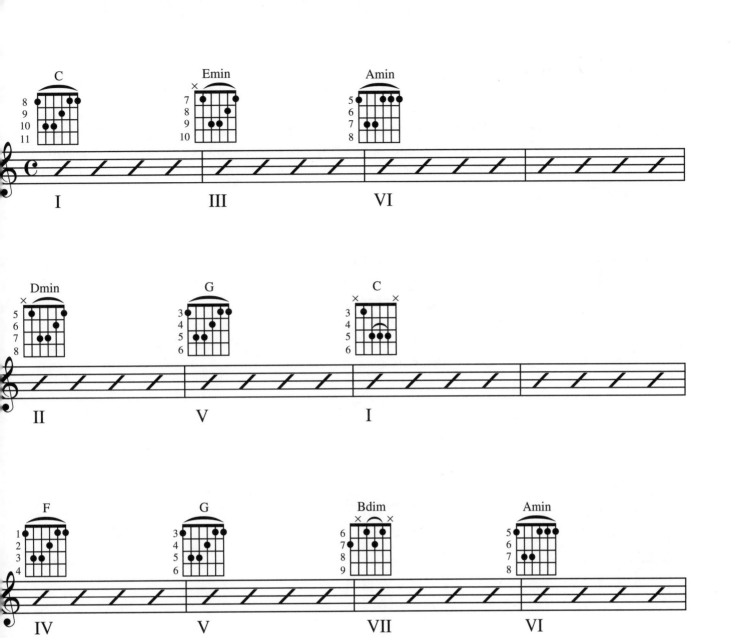

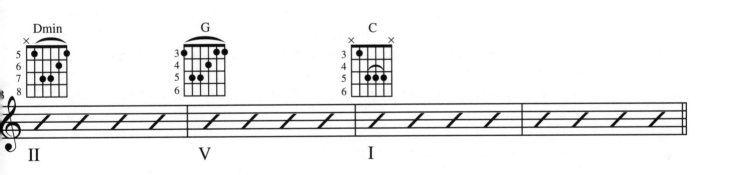

Diatonic 7th Chords

Now that you are accustomed to some diatonic sounds, let's expand on this idea.

Most of the previous diatonic chords are actually three-note chords called *triads*. In most cases you are probably strumming more than just three strings, but if you look carefully you will find that the chords really contain the same three notes duplicated two or more times. Look at the following examples.

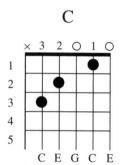

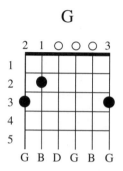

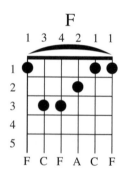

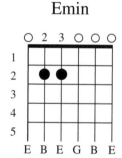

To make a slightly more sophisticated sound, we will often add a fourth note. These four-note chords are called 7th chords. This is because the fourth note we add will usually be the 7th note in the scale. No need to concern yourself with this for the moment, but if you find this interesting there are many books that explain this aspect of chord theory in detail (check out *Theory for the Contemporary Guitarist*, also published by the National Guitar Workshop and Alfred). For now, just learn these basics.

There will be new chord fingerings to learn, and these are provided within the examples on pages 86–87 and on pages 88–89. The diatonic 7th chords follow a similar pattern to that of the triads (pages 80–81). Notice that the only dominant 7 chord in a major key occurs on V.

I (1)   Major 7
II (2)   Minor 7
III (3)   Minor 7
IV (4)   Major 7
V (5)   Dominant 7
VI (6)   Minor 7
VII (7)   Minor 7♭5

The diatonic 7th chords for C Major are as follows.

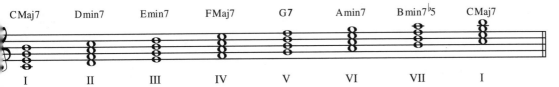

Here are the diatonic 7th chords for F Major.

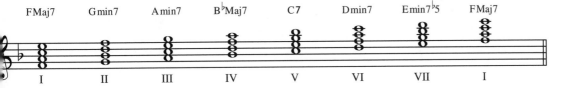

Here are the diatonic 7th chords for G Major.

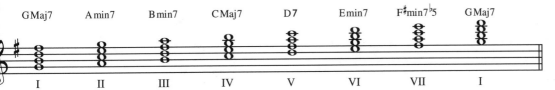

Here's a chart showing the diatonic 7th chords in all 12 keys.

KEY	DIATONIC 7TH CHORDS						
C	CMaj7	Dmin7	Emin7	FMaj7	G7	Amin7	Bmin7♭5
F	FMaj7	Gmin7	Amin7	B♭Maj7	C7	Dmin7	Emin7♭5
B♭	B♭Maj7	Cmin7	Dmin7	E♭Maj7	F7	Gmin7	Amin7♭5
E♭	E♭Maj7	Fmin7	Gmin7	A♭Maj7	B♭7	Cmin7	Dmin7♭5
A♭	A♭Maj7	B♭min7	Cmin7	D♭Maj7	E♭7	Fmin7	Gmin7♭5
D♭	D♭Maj7	E♭min7	Fmin7	G♭Maj7	A♭7	B♭min7	Cmin7♭5
G♭	G♭Maj7	A♭min7	B♭min7	C♭Maj7	D♭7	E♭min7	Fmin7♭5
B	BMaj7	C♯min7	D♯min7	EMaj7	F♯7	G♯min7	A♯min7♭5
E	EMaj7	F♯min7	G♯min7	AMaj7	B7	C♯min7	D♯min7♭5
A	AMaj7	Bmin7	C♯min7	DMaj7	E7	F♯min7	G♯min7♭5
D	DMaj7	Emin7	F♯min7	GMaj7	A7	Bmin7	C♯min7♭5
G	GMaj7	Amin7	Bmin7	CMaj7	D7	Emin7	F♯min7♭5

Diatonic 7th Chord Fingerings

Here are some more fingerings for diatonic 7th chords.

Set No. 1

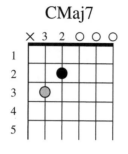

CMaj7

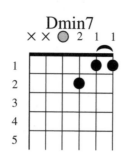

Dmin7

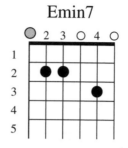

Emin7

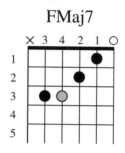

FMaj7

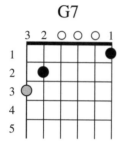

G7

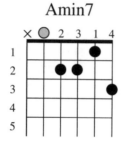

Amin7

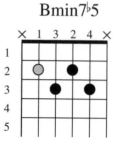

Bmin7♭5

Set No. 2

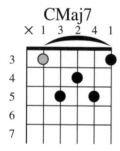

CMaj7

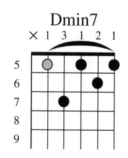

Dmin7

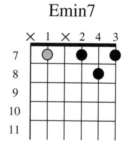

Emin7

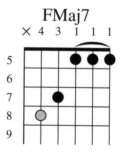

FMaj7

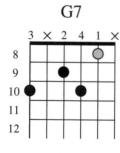

G7

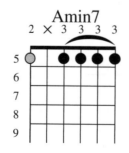

Amin7

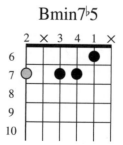

Bmin7♭5

GMaj7
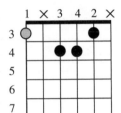

Amin7
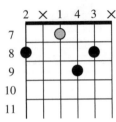

Bmin7
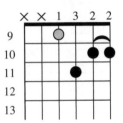

CMaj7
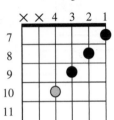

D7
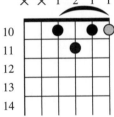

Emin7
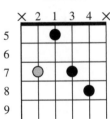

F♯min7♭5
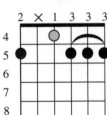

Here are the progressions from pages 82–83 again, this time using diatonic 7th chords in place of the diatonic triads.

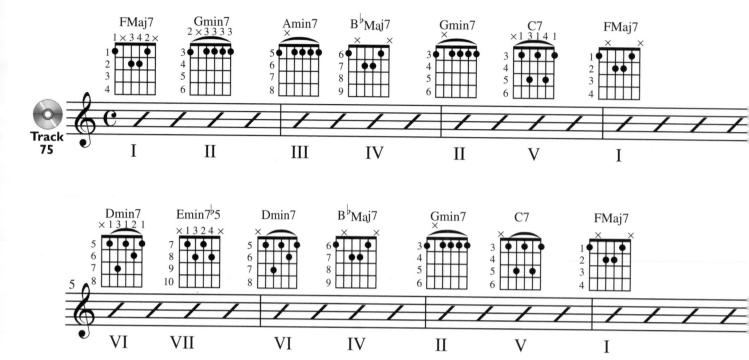

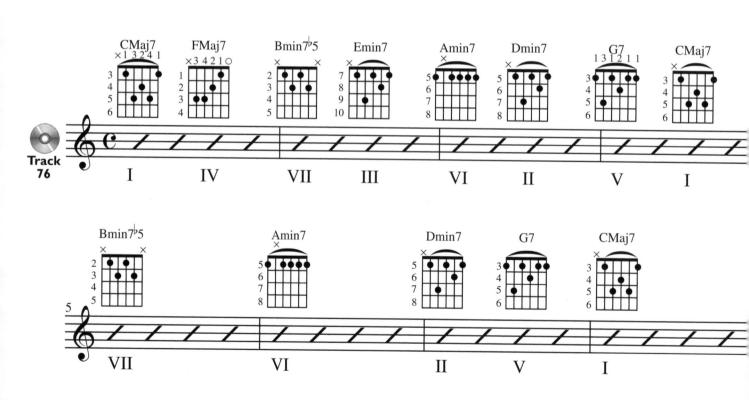

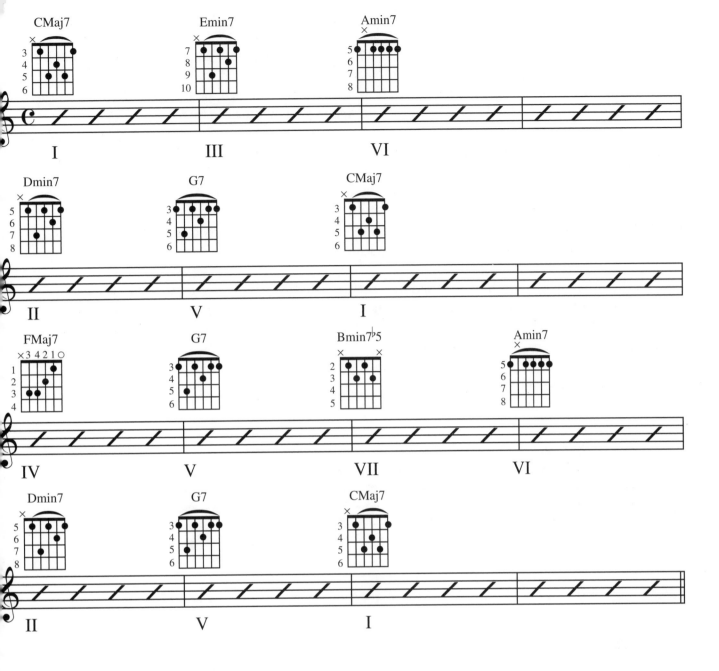

ere's your chance to get a little creative. Try replacing the triads in songs you know with their orresponding diatonic 7th chords.

iatonic Improvisation—Approach No. 1

nce you get a handle on these diatonic sounds, it's time to think about how you can improvise ver these types of chords and progressions. Once again, we are dealing with *progressional* nprovisation, meaning that a single scale can be used over an entire chord progression. vo approaches will be explained in this section. We will begin with the simplest approach.

ll of these diatonic chords are found naturally in the major scales. Since this is so, it stands to ·ason that we may use major scales for improvising. If the chords in a particular song are ·rived from a C Major scale, then all we have to do is use the C Major scale to improvise. kewise, you may use an F Major scale to improvise over the chords that come it, you can also ·se a G Major scale to improvise over the chords that come from it, and so on.

ow, you need only:

1. Be familiar with the diatonic chords of the keys in which you play most frequently.

2. Know some fingerings for the major scale.

Becoming familiar with the chords in a key is not difficult. The charts shown on pages 81 and 85 will help. Also, if you sing and play the guitar, it is quite possible that many of the songs you know are in the same few keys. If this is so, then sheer repetition will help acquaint you with the various chords found in those keys. Then you will need some major scale fingerings.

Major Scale Fingerings and Sample Solos

The major pentatonic scale you learned on page 74 will work beautifully over diatonic chord progressions in major keys. Simply match up the root of the major pentatonic scale to the key of the song you are playing. Use a C Major Pentatonic scale over the diatonic chords found in the key of C Major; use a D Major Pentatonic scale over the diatonic chords found in the key of D and so on. The same rule applies to the major scale.

Like all the other scales you have learned, the major scale fingerings shown here are moveable. You can move each pattern to any tonic you like. Use these in the same manner as the major pentatonic scale: match the tonic of the scale with the key of the song. Here are three major scale fingerings in C.

C Major Scale Fingerings

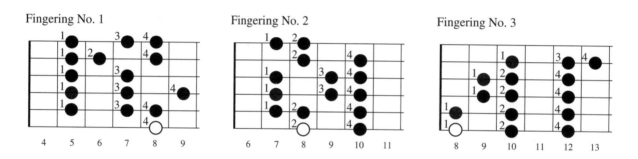

Fingering No. 1   Fingering No. 2   Fingering No. 3

Learning the following solos should help you get more familiar with the sound of soloing with the major scale. This first solo uses C Major Scale Fingering No. 1

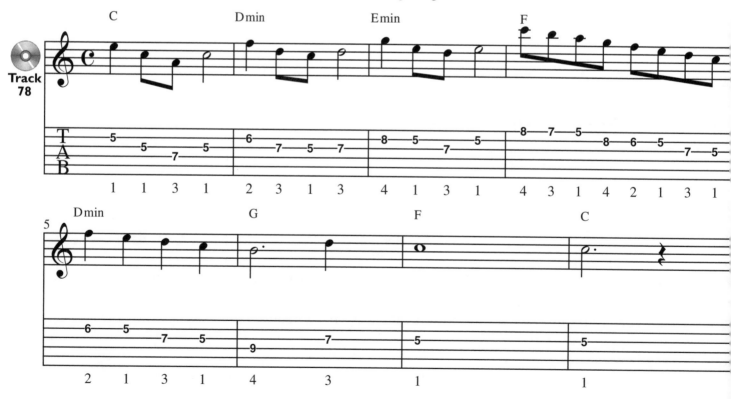

s solo uses C Major Scale Fingering No. 2

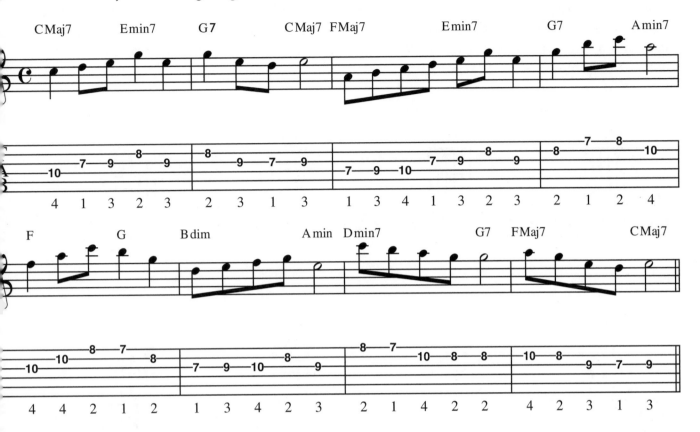

ally, here's an example of C Major Scale Fingering No. 3 at work.

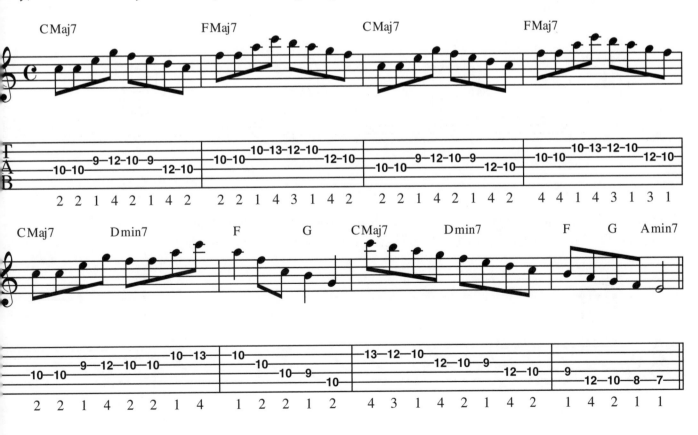

Here are some diatonic progressions for you to practice improvising over. You will find a rhythm guitar to play with on the CD included with this book. Or you can record yourself playing these progressions. The sounds of the major scale take a little longer to learn to manipulate than the major and minor pentatonic scales, but they will add a slightly more sophisticated musical element to your solos.

Use the C Major scale for the first two progressions.

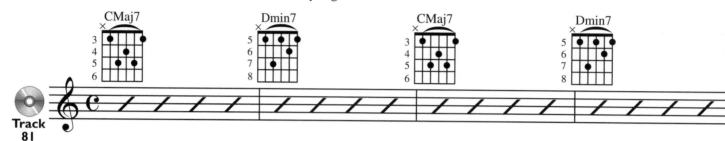

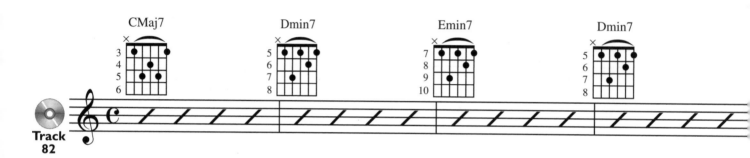

Use the F Major scale for this progression. Simply move the tonic of any C Major fingering to the note F, and off you go.

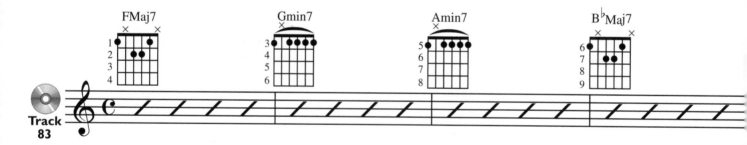

Since only the G Major scale will yield a D7 chord, that is the major scale to use here. Of course, either the D Major Pentatonic or D Minor Pentatonic scale would work too.

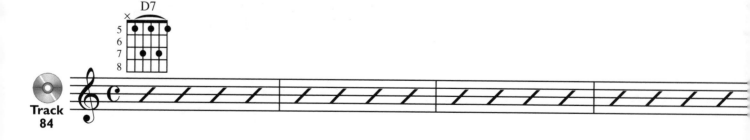

e the G Major scale to solo over this progression.

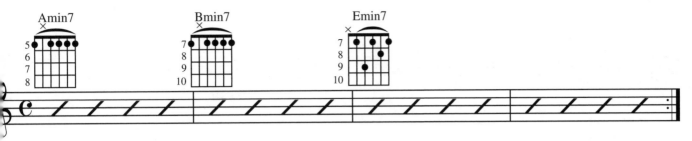

e the D Major scale for this one.

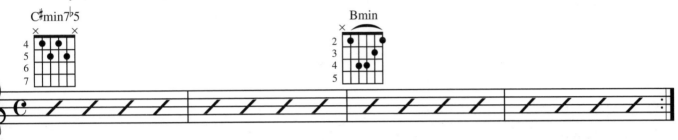

atonic Improvisation—Approach No. 2

proach No. 2 really is not that much different from Approach No. 1. You still need to know
diatonic chords and you still need to know your major scale fingerings. This approach helps
u handle improvising over progressions that contain chords from more than one key, which
ually describes most songs.

oking at the following chord progression, we see that there are chords from both the C Major
l F Major Scales. Here's a clue: There is no Gmin7 in the key of C Major! It isn't difficult to see
at the key has changed. Much of the time, it is the presence of a II–V–I progression that defines
ey. When playing over the chords in C, we use a C Major scale. When we get to the part of
e song where the chords are in F, we simply switch over to an F Major scale.

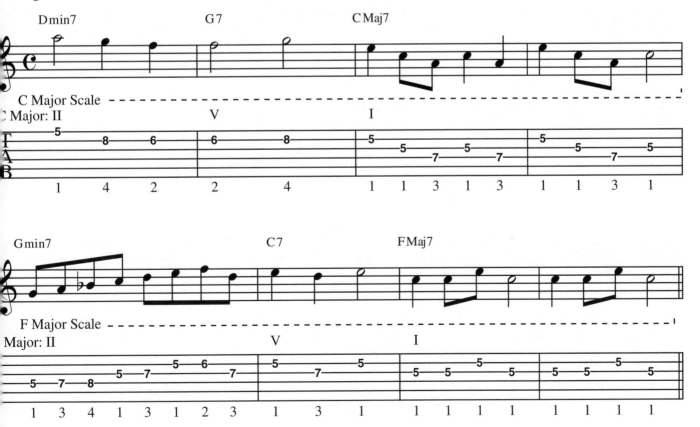

Here is another example using the same approach. This one moves from a G Major scale to a C Major scale.

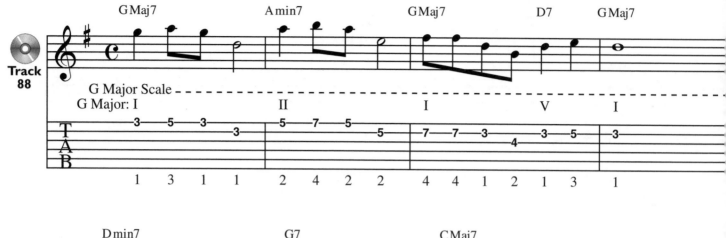

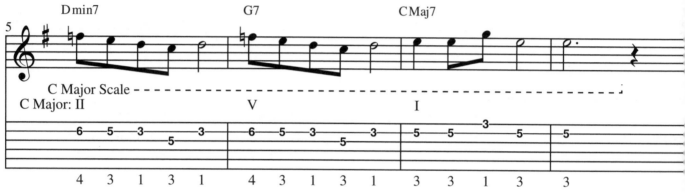

This one switches from F Major to B♭ Major.

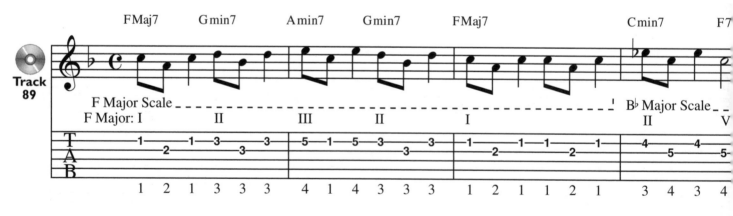

...eginning, if you only know one major scale fingering, you will have to move that
...g around the fretboard to match the various keys in which you are playing. As you
...e familiar with more fingerings, you won't have to jump around as much because an
...riate major scale fingering will always be close by.

...ese progressions to practice switching scales.

| G | C | G | C | Dmin7 | G7 | CMaj7 |

...Major Scale _ _ _ _ _ _ _ _ _ _ _ _ _ _ _ _ _ _ ⌐ C Major Scale _ _ _ _ _ _ _ _ _ _ _ _ _ ⌐
...ajor: I   IV   I   IV   C Major: II   V   I   (G Major: V)

(D7)

| Gmin7 | Amin7 |

Gmin7   Amin7   Gmin7   Amin7   Gmin7   Amin7

F Major Scale _ ⌐
...ajor: II   III

| Cmin7 | Dmin7 |

Cmin7   Dmin7   Cmin7   Dmin7   Cmin7   Dmin7

B♭ Major Scale _ ⌐
...ajor: II   III

| Dmin7 | G7 | CMaj7 | Fmin7 | CMaj7 |

...C Major Scale _ _ _ _ _ _ _ _ _ _ _ _ _ _ _ _ _ ⌐ E♭ Major Scale _ _ _ _ _ ⌐ C Major Scale _ _ _ _ _ ⌐
...Major: II   V   I   E♭ Major: II   C Major: I

Congratulations! You've done it. You've always said
...at you would come back to the guitar someday
...d—having gotten this far—it's likely that you're
...aying better than ever.

...on't stop now, this is just the beginning. At the right
...e some suggestions for perfect follow-ups to
...is book:

Beginning Jazz Guitar, Jody Fisher
Beginning Blues Guitar, David Hamburger
Beginning Rock Guitar, Paul Howard
Beginning Acoustic Guitar, Greg Horne
Beginning Fingerstyle Guitar, Lou Manzi

*All published by the National Guitar Workshop
and Alfred.*